REAL MEN

WHAT'S HAPPENING WITH OUR MEN?

A QuickRead by Greg E. Middleton

QUICKRead
SERIES

ISBN: 978-0-557-12071-0

DEDICATION

This book is dedicated to all men of all ages, races, nationalities, cultures, religions, or other distinctions and differences. There is a reason we were born male. That ultimate choice came from a Superior Power that intentionally made you the way you were designed to function. Don't take this responsibility lightly, because it is much different than what and how females were so uniquely designed to function. Males were designed to carry the weight of the species on their shoulders. When men fail, our species fails, and the world suffers greatly. We were designed to become the caretakers of this world. This current time is our leg of the journey. We must carry the torch while we are here and pass it on to the next generations of males. We must not fail nor belittle our mission. If we do, the consequences are far greater than we can imagine. "For God made man in His own image and likeness and gave him dominion over the earth." This book is dedicated to all of God's children, but specifically the males.

INTRODUCTION

What is a *real man*? Is there a particular image that comes to mind when you mention the term, *real man*? Depending upon your age and upbringing, you more than likely would have a very different image of what a *real man* looks and/or acts like. For example, a person born in 1990 would have a totally different impression of what a *real man* is compared to one born in 1930. The same would be true about a person born in the year 2000 as opposed to one born in 1900. Even though people are physically very much alike, things change around them that cause them to perceive life totally differently.

In 1900 things such as automobiles, airplanes, telephones, or televisions weren't even invented yet. Can you imagine life without such things? In 1950 there were no calculators, microwave ovens, or color televisions. Do you remember when the first home computer or mobile telephones first became available for the average consumer? So many things that we have grown accustomed to having are not all that old in terms of our human evolution. Just over the past one hundred years, life has changed so drastically that anyone fortunate enough to live a century would almost certainly feel like a fish out of water…in this 21st Century.

As we are experiencing life, things seem to move so gradually that you barely see the change. If you have ever watched a sunrise, you actually saw the movement of time as you witnessed the sun climbing up over the horizon. You see the light change from dim to full bright in just a few minutes. If you weren't consciously thinking about this daily event it could have easily passed you by unnoticed. Second after second, minute after minute, every hour, day, week, month and year, we see these subtle changes, yet we barely give them a second thought. We've become so conditioned to accepting change as an intricate part of life that it is no longer a conscious thought. Change and life are inseparable.

It's funny how time moves so slowly when you are young, but once you are older it appears to fly by. That is because the young are so eager to gain their adult independence and the old want so dearly to turn back the hands of time. Ironically, hardly anyone seems to be totally satisfied with their present. We're constantly looking at what we don't have rather than appreciating the *now* moment when things are actually happening.

In addressing the primary issues that seem to be plaguing males, we need only look at the nature of change. Time is automatic. It always does its job, but people seem to have a hard time making the proper adjustments to change. It's like watching a rapidly moving stream of water run down a city street and trying to guess the most appropriate time to jump in order to can get to the other side. The longer you wait, the harder it becomes to see the perfect moment to take the leap. Compare that stream with life. In life, we always have to make choices. Many times you don't have the luxury of waiting. Life is constantly in your face. As long as you are living you have to participate with what life issues to you. Although there are times when you may wish you could freeze time in order to allow the bad things to go away, that is not how life works. You must deal with the good and the bad. Life happens. We must participate in the happening.

Somehow it appears that for a stretch of time life was happening while men were adjusting to the shock of all the rapid changes. It feels as though men in general were placed behind the eight-ball – out of the sequence with life's flow. Many things changed so rapidly that it caught us off guard. We were forced to go along with numerous and drastic changes that we had never experienced before.

When women won their rights to become equal partners by law, rather than remaining the secondary partner, how did men adjust to the new law? Not well! They were no longer the undisputed heads of households, the primary wage earners, or the authoritative spokesman in the public eye. Beforehand, men were the ones who pulled all the strings as to how society operated. In essence, men had ruled (dominated) society with a heavy hand for centuries without challenge. When these laws suddenly changed, men did not know how to adjust to them. Although the law changed, and slowly the culture started changing, the minds and hearts of males did not follow suit. No one redefined the new role men should take in adjusting to the new female freedoms.

On the other hand, women had the law on their side. Even so, they still had to fight through the old culture, the status quo, and the stubborn hearts and minds of egotistic males who were not willing to give up their strangle hold on power. You had two opposing forces going in opposite directions; the stubbornness of males and the eagerness of women. Since the law was on the side of equality, there could only have been one winner. That fact did not mean the battle would be easy or quick. Even to this day, women are still fighting for equality and men still are not ready to give up their dominance.

Starting back in the 1920s, when women won the right to vote, things gradually began to change. The throne that men had sat on since the beginning of time started to corrode. Although it took many more years before women learned how to be heard publically and to acquire a public voice, the dethroning process essentially started with the voting act, continued on to the civil rights act of the 1960s, to this current day where things are not yet equal, but they certainly are a long ways from the days of unchallenged male domination.

Historians understand that each generation seems to have their unique challenges to overcome. Throughout the ages, mankind has had to deal with one obstacle after the next. Just when you thought things couldn't get worse, they got worse, but as a species we are survivors. We have learned to overcome the mightiest of challenges life has tossed at us, and yet we are still thriving. Our numbers have always been increasing since the beginning. Where there have been potholes, we found a way to get around them. Through wars, sicknesses, plagues, droughts, storms, famine, horrendous fires, meteor storms, global warming, ice ages, torrential floods, earthquakes, and the like, we not only survived, but thrived as a species.

Even though the situation with males may have been damaged, time and evolution seem to have a conscious mind of their own. When the dinosaurs were no longer necessary, they became extinct and turned into fossil fuel that we use today to run our motor vehicles. Whenever a species ceases to serve a worthy function they become extinct. It is the way of all matter and energy in the natural realm. Things may change or evolve, but nothing is ever completely lost. It merely converts into another form and continues eternally. In the universe nothing is really lost. It is a constant recycling of energy and matter. Although changes may seem insurmountable, they are merely steps along the way of eternal evolution. Life continues to exist after making the necessary adjustments.

No matter how odd the situation seems, particularly for males in our current-day society, the byproduct is what the universe is forming from what we brought to the table. In spite of our free will and our corruptible nature, we are not consciously powerful enough to override the grand scheme of the universe. In fact, we are only a tiny grain of sand on the beachfront of the entire universe. There is a power that is far greater than us keeping things moving through the millenniums in a predictable manner, which we do not fully understand. If you're worried about the status of our world, I wouldn't lose too much sleep over it. In the end things will migrate and transcend into the higher universal order. The question is; what will become of us?

In the meantime, what are we going to do about the role of males in our current-day society? Are we to take a back seat and allow the hands of evolution to produce something better, or is it up to us to pay attention to the hints that life gives us and make necessary changes according to what we can clearly see is broken? Life has given us very clear signals that we are sliding down a very slippery slope that may alter our species in how things are done. If things continue on their current path, women will become the dominant gender and men will be forced to take the back seat. Perhaps it is time for the females to take the lead role in humanity for a change. Males certainly dominated our world all these years, and look at what we have to show?

Perhaps females need a chance to show us a more sensitive and compassionate way of doing things. If females were our leaders, would they be as eager to send our sons and daughters into war or otherwise put them in harm's way without trying every other alternative first? Perhaps we need a change in how we do things? We have become too hostile and too quick to wage war rather than exhausting other methods of resolving our conflicts. We are not as loving, kind, or caring enough of each other.

Would females be as ruthless if they were in the leadership position? The jury is still out.

One thing we know for certain is that change, even though it is not always welcomed, is necessary. As creatures of habit, our basic human nature compels us to hang on, even to our dysfunctional habits – knowing they are no longer working. In order to break a bad habit, one must create separation from the old one by using an overwhelming force. Once the old is gone, it has to be replaced by the new. People even rejected the locomotive engines that replaced the horse and buggy. They opposed the internet that replaced the postal mail system. Change is not always readily accepted, but usually when the dust settles, the benefits prevail. Have males come to such a fork in the evolution of time?

The bottom line is that we really need to talk about this "male thing." Something is not right about how males are operating in our current society. Although many of the recent changes were necessary, men need to make the proper adjustments and stand back up at the plate – taking their rightful position in society. When the dust finally settles, where will men stand? Is the new *real man* the same image as it was once thought to be? This is the subject of this book. What is a real man?

Contents

REAL MEN

WHAT'S HAPPENING WITH OUR MEN

Greg E. Middleton

PREFACE

I'm a firm believer in all things happening in their intended time and space. Even though we have a bit of latitude and leverage with the use of our power of free will, when the dust settles, things tend to work out as they should. One might say, "As they were intended." This does not mean that all of life is already a foregone conclusion or that we should just sit back and watch it happen. It simply means that life is far more sophisticated than we could possibly imagine. It already knows what is going to happen, and yet it still makes it appear as though we actually made it happen. We are "one" with life. Life dances with us! As we are moving and breathing it is dancing with us - giving us the impression that we are actually in the lead position, but in actuality, it feeds us our thoughts so it knows what we are about to do. All living things are attached to a stream of consciousness that flows throughout the universe and guides all things in the manner in which they were intended. In essence, life is a conscious notion.

You may disagree with this thought, but in an attempt to prove it wrong, go out and see if you can change the fate of the world. Nothing you can do would change the universe to the point that you would actually cause it to become something totally different. Life has been around far longer than we have. In fact, we are merely passing through its vast networks. The universe has been fully operating without our presence for billions of years. You didn't cause any of this to happen. In fact, you are merely a product of what was caused by this Power that originated all things.

The fact that this book is coming to you now means that it was time for it to be written, published, and made available to get into your hands. The idea for this book originally came to me back in 2003 or 2004, but it was not time for it to be manifested back then. Although I knew something was wrong with how males were handling things, and that something had shifted in the way our lives were unfolding, at the time I could not fully express what I was sensing in words. I started a men's meeting group in order to discuss the male issues and called it *Real Men Seminars*. I only wanted to gather as many men together as I could in order to figure out our current situations. What I did not know at the time was the fact that I was not ready to write the book, or run an organization dealing specifically with male issues. I wasn't fully prepared by the universe to bring forth that message.

In the spring of 2007 I was diagnosed with prostate cancer. This is a very common problem for many men my age and race, but I knew very little about it. While going through the process, I had to learn so much about this ailment, because my operation was not administered properly - causing other complications with my male functions. After going through the many problems and procedures, I was actually being prepped to lead a men's group - discussing male issues. This was only a part of life's plan for me. It was nothing I planned or manipulated in any way, but it was the plan life (God, the universe) chose for me. Even the ability to write started about ten years back, as this power began teaching me how to write down messages. God had a plan for me and His plan unfolded right before my own eyes, but far beyond my absolute control.

The information you are about to read was forged in me from some universal power and somehow sent through me to deliver unto you. I think it is just a wakeup call to men. Wakeup my brothers!

Chapter One

THE NATURAL DESIGN

There is no question that males have dominated the human race since the beginning of time. Yes, this has been a man's world with women as a secondary partner. Things have never been equal for both sexes in terms of rights, power, or privileges. It is fairly obvious that males and females were either designed or created differently by way of purpose and intent. It is also as obvious that there were other factors at hand that determined the distribution of power between the sexes. We clearly see that the average human male was given superior brute physical strength over his female counterpart, but was that power intended to be used to overpower females against their will?

One could argue that Mother Nature (God or a superior power) rarely makes mistakes regarding her plans and intent, because things tend to work in a manner in which they were naturally designed to operate. If we believe males were built to dominate – that is what has indeed unfolded over the years. No one would argue the point that males were created or designed larger by accident. All things in life tend to serve a definite purpose. The fact that the average male is notably larger than the average female reveals a purpose within itself. No one had to tell the first males to go out and start hunting and gathering food. That instinct was built within the primary design. Likewise, no one has to tell a bird to fly or a fish to swim. That ability is built within them.

However, especially with human beings, the element of freewill is not necessarily within the control of natural design. Given the choice, human beings seem to go against what is natural, right, practical, or even what is more beneficial. It is not uncommon for people to make choices that may work against themselves. In essence, the element of free will seems to trump the natural design when the desire is present for selfish gain. Naturally, men having the superior physical power

1

took control simply because they could. Women were in second position because they didn't have the necessary power to resist man's control.

If you approach the subject from a spiritual or religious point of view, it is said that God created man in His image and appointed man to be the head of the human family. Regardless of your stance, it is still obvious that man became the head of the human race because he was designed that way. Even so, this still does not account for the fact that, given the opportunity, people tend to take advantage of whatever distinct advantage they have over another.

In our early days, brute strength was a dominant factor. That was then, but we live in a totally different world today where mere brute strength no longer carries as much significance as before. Today we have placed our power in things, warfare, money, psychological control, caste systems, and the like. Even the mighty Sampson from the biblical stories would have to bow before a 90-pound man with an Uzzy today. Brute strength is no longer the order of the day. Having a distinct advantage over another is the new order.

Before we get deeply engrossed into this subject, there are a few questions you need to consider. Has there been a drastic shift in the male/female dynamic over the past century? Are we satisfied with the way things have progressed? Has the new role of males in our society been clearly defined?

If you are very satisfied with the status quo, then this subject may not be of interest to you. However, if you see the need to make some alterations in how this issue is being postulated, perhaps you may want to engage, if for no other reason than for your own understanding. By knowing where you stand and understanding how you got there, it is easier to make changes, if that is your desired goal. If you see a shift in how males operate and are treated in this new age, you may want to take a look at the past in order to make the proper adjustments so you may improve the present, and secure the future.

PICK YOUR PATH

When it comes to the natural design there are basically two different camps from which to choose. One is the *Theory of Evolution* and the other is the *Creation Theory*. The first postulates that all life evolved into what we have become and the second states that we were created to become as we have. Obviously, there are some that take neither side and just accept what *is*, regardless of how it got here. It is important to note that how we perceive things can be a factor in how we operate within our perceived knowledge. This is especially true regarding the subject of the male/female dynamic.

If you believe in the *Creation Theory* you more than likely accept the fact that God made man (males) to be the head of the human family structure. Most major worldwide religions will teach that position. If you hold that to be true, then more than likely that belief would have a major impact upon how you deal with the male/female dynamic. You would also need to factor the strength of your belief into the equation. Even in accepting such a hypothesis as your truth, you still have the power to ignore it and operate as though it doesn't matter. There are many who claim to believe in God and understand His rules and/or boundaries yet live as though it doesn't matter. What does that say about beliefs? If you have the power to go against what you feel to be right or true, then what does that say about you? Such questions take us far deeper into the subject matter than most are willing to entertain. Nonetheless, if such questions are not answered, one could never be certain of exactly where they stand on the issue.

Our beliefs are a major part of our operating systems. What we believe to be true or false, whether real or unreal, matters. What we accept as laws, rules, agreements, or boundaries guide us in the decisions we make. Those who believe in a divine power, such as God, are driven by what they believe to a certain extent, even if it is only in their subconscious mind. Feeling guilty when you cross a boundary line is a factor of how the subconscious mind works. When you ignore or otherwise break a known law, or steal from someone knowing it is wrong, your subconscious mind will send you an uncomfortable signal. However, if you do this on a regular basis, you learn to ignore that subconscious voice of reasoning.

The point is, just because we know what is right or wrong, or perceive it to be so, doesn't necessarily make us abide within those parameters. Even though, such things may influence you to various degrees, they are not absolute. When you apply this unnatural inner contradiction to the male/female dynamic, you can see how our will power (volition) can and many times does trump the natural design. In reality this is not just a case of the contrasting theories of our existence - it is more about how we choose to operate with our power of free will (volition). Being a religious person does not necessarily make one do what is rational, right, reasonable, or beneficial. At the same time, believing in the *Theory of Evolution* does not make one a worse person as far as how they operate within society. In order to affectively deal with the male/female dynamic, one must decide within them self what matters. If treating people fair is part of your core value, then it shouldn't matter if the person is male or female. Fairness becomes the issue over gender. If a person is mean-spirited they usually apply it to everyone. The only difference is the fact that they tend to apply it more to those they have more leverage over in order to get away with it.

MARS AND VENUS CONCEPT

Much has been written and spoken about the differences between how males and females operate. It is not by accident that we have a different basic operating system. For example, we build motor vehicles as a means of transportation. We build calculators to assist us in computing numerical equations. One would not expect a calculator to serve as a means of transportation because it was not built for that purpose. In a broader sense, men and women were designed (built) for different purposes. From a design prospective, women were given operating systems to enhance the purposes of which they were created (built): Men were likewise.

For example, women were given the ability to conceive and have babies. They were also given the trait of nurturing and caring for their young. Part of their traits and operating systems were built around their design and purpose. This is not to say that women were only built for the purpose of having babies, it means that it is a unique function to them that men do not have. Since this function is unique to females, it is only natural that men are not equal to women in such capacities. Men were built to serve other functions within the human species of which the protectors and providers were arguably two of the traits that were uniquely designed within them. This does not mean that women cannot be good providers or protectors of the family, but that certain traits within their operating systems were not specifically geared for that purpose. Regardless as to how we choose to operate within humanity, we cannot ignore the fact that certain traits seem to be more prevalent in a particular gender than in the other.

Even in stating this supposition, it does not mean that people can't do as they choose. This is where free will comes into play. There are times when necessity makes the choice against what one may wish or hope to choose otherwise. With single-parent families on the rise many females are left with the total burden of raising and providing for their children. Regardless to what is natural, or the intended design specifications, once children are born into the world someone has to provide, care, protect, nurture, and otherwise raise them. In the absence of having both male and female guardians someone will have to do what is necessary. One gender, usually the female, will have to assume both roles and do as best as they can under the circumstances. Even though it may not have been a conscious choice to be in that situation, necessity dictates a different set of rules that must be obeyed.

In reference to the natural design regarding gender differences, we must understand that even though the design was different and the roles and purposes were different, at the end of the day, necessity and free will dominates the table. Understanding the differences between the natural, unique designs of the genders should assist us in relating to each other and affectively doing the jobs we find before us. Understanding your function and carrying out that purpose is part of your birthright. How you carry out your particular assignment is personal. It has a lot to do with the authentic person that resides in your shell called a human being. Even though we may not realize it, or consciously know it to be true, there is a power and a force in the universe that is far greater than we are. Individually we will die at a given point, but life carries on. A question we should inquire of ourselves is, when that final breath is taken, did you do your best with the plate that was placed before you.

Although this topic is specifically geared toward defining a real man, on a wider view we should be looking at becoming the most genuine person we are capable of being. With that as our primary goal, our natural given abilities will excel in the manner in which they were intended. Gender should not be an issue that we allow to create separation or dissention. Males and females were built for one another, as a hand and glove, to be the caretakers of this planet. If we abide by the natural order it will serve us well. If we do not, then the consequences will be on our shoulders.

Chapter Two

WHAT MAKES US MEN

Without getting into the religious aspects of our anatomy, let's view this subject from a neutral, universal position. From what we can tell in all the known universe there are polar opposites. Everything that exists needs its opposite in order to sustain existence. In reality, there cannot be one without the other. Just think rationally for a moment regarding the things you know to exist; think of their polar opposite. For hot there is cold, north there is south, up is down, left is right, wrong is right, heads is tails, tall is short, inside and outside, light and dark, positive is negative, and for male there is female. This is not a scientific theory, but as you think about it – can you think of anything that does not have an opposite? Even matter has antimatter. The scientific theory of relativity states that for every action there is an equal and opposite reaction. It seems that for everything to exist it needs a counterbalancing force in order to support its existence. Since there are only two genders in the human race, they support each other in universal existence. I'm sure there is a more scientific version of this supposition, but for now we can accept the fact that males and females partly compose the yin and yang of the universe. Not only do we support each other, we are also the other half that make each other complete.

As mentioned earlier, each gender seems to have a specific design and intended purpose. Without getting heavily into all the technical specifics, we can agree that human males carry or create the sperm that is required in order for procreation, and the females carry the required egg. Although these are not the only differences, we can all agree on these two. We also can agree that *at birth* only the male has a penis, testicles, and the prostate gland; while the female has a clitoris, vagina, and ovaries. These unique parts of our anatomy came with the design package and make us uniquely either male or female. These are just a few of the physical differences between males and females. However, in addition to the purely physical differences, there are mental and emotional differences that are likewise built within the design. Apparently, each sex is wired differently according to their intended design function.

Studies have shown that certain abilities or traits are attached to a particular part of our brains. For example, the ability to hunt or otherwise gather food or sustenance is stored in a particular part of the male brain. It also shows that the trait of nurturing and tending to the needs of children is attached to a particular part of the female brain. In each gender the brains are wired differently by design. Arguably, that tells us that we were designed, created, made, or evolved in a uniquely different way in order to fulfill specific functions and/or purposes. This is not an argument regarding what one does with their unique anatomy by way of sexual preferences or choices. It is merely an acknowledgment that we have different anatomies that serve specific purposes. For all intents and purposes, the different anatomies are a part of what makes one either male or female, but our anatomy is not the only thing that makes a male what we call a man. In today's medical technology the anatomy can be altered.

When it comes to our anatomy, very few would disagree about our uniqueness, which appears to be attached to certain specific gender purposes. What seems to be more at issue is how our differences may have been used to place certain parties in a disadvantaged position, or to discriminate against a person because of their inherit design or personal preferences. It takes more than just the anatomy to make one a *real man* or a *real woman*. This is partly because of how society has defined the gender roles. It is also partly in how we have been conditioned to accept these unique boundary roles.

Our conditioning tells us that a person with a certain anatomy and of a certain age legally becomes a man or a woman. Although legally and anatomically that may be true, we also understand that if one does not act or fulfill a certain role or image as designated by the populace, they may not be acknowledged as a *real man, or woman*. Using this criteria, it is not just the anatomy or the natural selection that makes one a *real man*. In addition, it also requires fulfilling a certain predetermined function and purpose in order to be acknowledged as a *real man*. Moreover, merely having a surgical sex change or electing to live one's life as the opposite gender does not change who they were born to be. It only changes their appearance and preference. Inwardly they are still the same soul.

For the sake of this topic, "What makes us male," let us leave sexual preferences out of the equation for now. How a person lives their lives or alters their anatomy is not the issue this book is attempting to cover. Genes and DNA never change. Alternatively, this topic is specifically discussing what we are willing to categorize as a *real man*. More specifically, we are addressing this subject from a pre-designed purpose and/or "intent" point of view. What is it that distinguishes a male (man) from the female (woman)? Is it mere anatomy, character, strength, heart, responsibility, or what? Rather than thinking scientifically or super analytically, think in more *common sense* terms. What functions do males play in society?

Arguably a *real man* is one who assumes the role as a wonderful father to his children, regardless of the circumstances. He serves, protects, provides, cares for, cherishes, honors, respects, and loves all of who are placed under his paternal responsibilities. In fact, he places their welfare before his own selfish desires. A *real man* never does things that he knows would cause harm to those who are dependent on him. He would never abuse them in any way knowingly. He would never abandon them or otherwise place them in harm's way. He would be willing to give of himself, including his very life, in order to protect and serve those under his care. On a broader scale, all the people that come in contact with him would be blanketed by all he knows as a functioning male. Integrity does not draw a line at blood relations; it extends into infinity. A *real man* is one of integrity, truth, honor, and high moral character.

Even though this characterization of a *real man* may sound unrealistic, noble, or too moralistic, what trait mentioned above would any man want to ignore regarding his loved ones? Would he wish they depended upon him less or offered them less than his best? This is what each man has to answer in his heart and mind. Integrity is certainly one of the main characteristics of a *real man*.

9

Although I cannot speak for the majority of the males, our written laws, customs, and adopted morals speak for themselves. We (Americans) are a nation of laws and rules that were supposedly written under godly principles according to our constitution. If that document is not something that we are willing to honor then what's the point? Either we are what we claim to be, or not! As of late, such principles seem to be more optional than the expected norm. Do we still even believe in those principles that were established hundreds of years ago? If not, we need to state what principles we are willing to honor. If we are a nation of laws, it should be ones that we are willing to honor.

One of the most important traits of a *real man* other than integrity is being *authentic*. Such a man is truthful from the inside out. You can only get out of something that is already contained within. You can't get blood out of a turnip unless you first put it in there. Truth needs to be at the core of a man first and foremost. Being true to one's self (your intents and purposes) is the hallmark of a *real man*. If that solid connection is not there, how can anyone be anything real?

PERCEPTION VERSUS REALITY

It is fairly obvious that our overall perception of things does not match the reality we are experiencing. This is primarily because society has changed so drastically. Nonetheless, the hearts and minds of most men are still trapped in the past. At issue here is bringing our perceptions up to date in order to match our reality in this new 21st Century. Life has changed so much since the days when women were expected to stay at home to raise the children and have dinner ready when the man came home from a hard day at the job. That stereotype is no longer the *norm*. In today's family many women are spending the same amount of time at the job and are equally as tired when they come home to the family. Does that mean that we should always expect women to still do all the cooking and cleaning (woman's work) regardless of the new circumstances? If our perception of the role of a wife still defines her as the official homemaker of the family, in spite of her additional duties as a co-financial provider, does that create a happy wife? Would it not be the right human thing to do that her husband pitch in and help to the best of his abilities with whatever chores must be done?

Who was it that determined cooking and cleaning the house to be exclusively women's work regardless of the situation? Couples should come together as a family unit and discuss how they wish to distribute the chores and responsibilities, rather than trying to adhere to a system that no longer works. Following traditions for the sake of "tradition" solves nothing, nor does it make a happy and harmonious family.

Our understanding of the roles of males and females in a marriage are old and antiquated. Regardless of what our traditions may say, people have to live together on a daily basis and maintain the integrity of the family unit. When certain expectations were set years ago, most women did not venture into the workplace daily. Most were stay-at-home housewives who accepted that role within the family structure. Since the laws have changed giving women equal access to the workplace, including jobs with salaries that may surpass her mate, that old rule should no longer apply.

Suppose the husband stays at home all day and cares for the children while the wife is out at work. Should he wait on her to come home to do the cooking and cleaning as well? If you look at this from a human prospective it seems only right that each party should do what is necessary for the good of the team. Couples should sit down and talk about what works best for their family, rather than trying to follow an antiquated concept that no longer works. A *real man* would understand this and do what is right without trying to stick to ineffective perceptions that no longer work.

THEN AND NOW

As you mature in life you may find that your experiences are usually far different from that of your father's, even though he may have been the one who trained you to act and operate as you do. To understand this better, take the analogy of a seasonal fruit tree. Each year a mature fruit tree will blossom and produce a new crop. Even though it is the same tree, each crop is different. Although the fruit may be very similar to the previous crop in many aspects, it is truly different simply because of the differences in the elements that factored into the production of the fruit. The amount of water, sunlight, pollination, and other natural factors combined to make each crop unique within itself.

In a similar manner, we may come from a very similar source, but the elements that combine in order to produce us were different from those before us. Look at how siblings from the same mother and father can be so different. Even though there may be many similarities, there are also so many differences. Because of the variances we are truly different fruit from our parents, siblings, or any other human being. In addition to the elements of nature, we also have to factor in how time is continually moving, which causes all things to change as well.

Many people will try to use the past in order to compare themselves with what may have happened previously. Although this may be a good benchmark to use as a foundation, it is not the actual foundation. You may learn from it, both what to, or not to do, but you can't become it. The past <u>was</u>, but it <u>is</u> no more. Apparently the universe spawns us as unique individuals intended to fulfill a specific function and purpose within a specific and unique time slot. We can never become an exact duplicate of the past, nor were we intended to be. As we know life to be ever progressing, our goal should always be to seek improvement upon what came before us. At times the standards seemed to have been set very high and unreachable. We should use that as our motivation, not as an albatross.

On the practical and literal side, the past is forever gone. It shall never be again. Imagine the life you are seeing today compared to people who were living just one hundred years ago. The things that you are witnessing were not even imaginable then. The things that your grandchildren will see cannot even be imagined now. It is fruitless to even attempt to re-live the past because that would be like reading yesterday's headlines. Things have moved on. People have passed away. All we have is the present moment, with the ability to do our absolute best right now. If you don't like the world you see, then do your part to change it. Start by changing yourself – if you are willing to admit that you need changing.

Chapter Three

TELL ME SOMETHING I DON'T KNOW

As you look deeply into this subject regarding the male position within society, you will begin to see it as an individual problem that affects the masses. Even though we are the human race, and specifically the male portion of our race, in reality we are individuals dealing with the complexity of the whole. If you see the Great Wall of China, it is composed of millions and millions of individual bricks. If one brick was defected, the wall would still stand, but the wall cannot necessarily save that one brick from destruction. In essence, each brick needs to stand on its own within the collection. The wall will be fine as it has been for thousands of years.

Each man is just like that one-brick-in-the-wall. As a gender we have done fine. We are still standing relatively strong, even though many of our individual members are defected and falling into destruction. Even though our combined mass has the ability to help save individuals, that is not something we have done well..., at least not up to this date. Apparently, our pride and egos are too inflated to admit that we have a weakness, so we don't seek the aid of each other. At issue with most males is the inability to admit or express a problem. Because of this, so many serious needs are hidden behind a superior force known as *male pride*. This is actually false pride fueled by perceived egos. Nothing about this behavior is real except the results.

On the other hand, females are extremely good at speaking with each other about things that bother them. They are not afraid to talk about emotional problems, admit sickness or weaknesses, or talk about whatever may be on their minds. Because of this ability to freely express themselves with each other, females get the much needed help they require from each other. There is no reason that males should not be able to achieve the same benefits from each other. This has to change if we are to become healthy bricks in the wall of humanity. We cannot allow our pride and egos to hold us back from becoming our best. Even though the average male is not geared toward gossip and idle chatter, they should be geared toward doing what is best in order to achieve the highest benefit. This does not mean that men should become more like women in this regard, but that they should look at the picture with the end result in mind, rather than what pride or ego demands.

♀

FALSE PERCEPTIONS AND PERSECUTION

Back in the day when a boy was slight of frame, spoke with a high pitched voice, or otherwise showed feminine traits, they were severely ostracized. If they did not match up to the standard of someone's interpretation of masculinity, (including their father's) they were teased or taunted. Since peer pressure has always been a major factor of our self esteem, many boys were severely wounded by such off-the-wall comments. No puns intended, but look at the off-the-wall comments directed at the late Michael Jackson. Was he not destroyed internally by what he had to deal with as a growing boy-child? It may be hard for us to feel sorry for him because of all his great accomplishments, but inside the man there were many deep emotional scars that may have been a contributing cause of his early death. Fortunately for Michael, he was able to take those scars and turn them into something great. When you have lemons - make lemonade. Unfortunately, not everyone has that unique ability. Most people who are severely scarred emotionally do not have the capacity or ability to turn it into something good. In such cases, wouldn't it be nice if the wall could reach down and lift up some of its bricks?

The irony of the situation is that we all know such things, but something keeps us from doing something about what we know. It is not just the pride and ego, but more the peer pressure of stepping outside the *norm* and doing something about what everyone knows. Do you remember earlier in the career of Mike Tyson when he was on top of the boxing world? We watched him make mistake after mistake in his personal life, but it seems that no one was there to tell him what apparently everyone knew, but him. Consequently, he kept on making mistakes until perhaps the consequences of his actions forced a change. This comment is not intended to belittle or judge Mike Tyson, but merely to point out how we allow things to happen right under our noses and do nothing. Perhaps someone did attempt to grab Mike and tell him these things, but he was not ready to hear them. When you are rich and famous, many people will ignore your dysfunctional behaviors in exchange for the privilege of being able to hang with someone rich and famous. When you are up on top everybody loves you, but when you fall back into the pack you suddenly become that ordinary person that gets very little attention from anyone. This is just the way we are as human beings. It is a flaw in our basic human nature.

HUMAN NATURE

In looking at our situation and trying to analyze the potential culprits, we cannot overlook our basic human nature. Earlier we spoke about free will, which is volition. Part of being human is having the ability to make certain choices as we wish. This has little to do with abilities, capabilities, talents, gifts, socio-economic backgrounds, educational background, race, culture, or other human distinction. Free will stands alone outside most other distinguishing characteristics.

Every day of our lives we have to make many choices about life itself. Some choose to get out of bed and do things, while others choose to do nothing. People choose to speak intelligently, harshly, kind, or rudely with one another. They can be generous, courteous, mean, hateful, or loving to one another. We have the ability to choose who we want to show a particular behavior toward or we can simply ignore people.

Just because we have almost countless choices, doesn't mean we should carry them out. When you are in a lower position (less powerful) you may not be able to enforce your wishes. When you are in a higher position (more powerful) you may be able to push your weight over others. Having choices does not guarantee you the ability to enforce them; neither does it ensure that they will be good or beneficial ones. Such things are more determined by our ability to control our basic human nature.

By understanding our ordinary human nature we realize that things such as character, attitude, and behavior were not necessarily traits we were born with. We developed such mannerisms as we were indoctrinated by our environment. If you take a human child and have it raised by a gorilla family, that child would be much different than one raised by human parents, even though he could have been produced by a mother and father with great genes. Many of our traits are learned. Children imitate what they see and hear. If they are placed around high and noble characteristics chances are they will express such behavior - in the absence other compelling factors.

A human being is like an empty canvass that began taking its shape long before it was given birth into the world. In their mother's womb, the canvass starts receiving instructions. The color, gender, hair color, eyes, features, genetic structure, DNA composition, and so many other characteristics were painted on the canvass long before the child materialized through the birth cannel. After the child is born, the painting continues on indefinitely until the person dies. The many factors that mold us into the people we become are so complicated that it can never be duplicated exactly. Every human being is truly one of a kind. When you separate the males from the females you will find many similarities within the genders, but still there are so many variations that contributed to how each particular canvass was painted. For this reason, attempting to place all males in one category, and all females in another, is impossible. However, even with that said there still are some notable similarities within the sexes.

MALE TENDENCIES

Before we talk about the typical male behavior, let's first dismiss the normal stereotyping. Males come in all shapes and forms. We are not creatures who run in packs, even though some of our behaviors may lead someone to think so. Similar to canines having alpha dogs (the natural leaders of the pack), we also have alpha males. You will know them when you see them. Some men are natural leaders and some only want to fit into the back of the pack. Some are hound dogs and some are not. Some are quite chauvinistic and others not. Some are well mannered, well groomed, house trained, and some not. Some know absolutely nothing about chivalry, courtesy, and honor, and some are knights in shining armor. For women to group us all under one pack – think again! We realize that not all women are the same, so give us that same benefit of the doubt until one of us proves otherwise. It is best to be only thought of as an idiot rather than open our mouths and remove all doubt.

TYPICAL MALE NOTIONS

1. When we are with our ladies we typically like to lead from the front, but if she's fine enough, we really don't have a problem bringing up the rear.
2. We really don't like being told what to do in a condescending tone by our mates. Our mothers did that to us when we were boys, but we knew we had nothing but love for her, so it wasn't a big deal. Even to this day, she can still talk to us like that and we still know we love her, but that position was earned.
3. Guys really need some space being alone to breathe, think, fart, or otherwise stretch it out. If they are not given the space, they feel like a caged animal waiting on the first opportunity to cut loose. This is called cave time by Dr. Gray.
4. Guys like hanging out with each other, not because they are gay, but because they understand the same dysfunctional language. At times we don't even need to use words to get our message across. Yea...it's like that...kool-man-kool...
5. Try leaving the fixing to us when possible. Our brains are normally made like that. Even if we don't know what we are doing, play along with us before you cut us down. We don't like our egos bruised too often.
6. Most men need some activity to play hard, rough, or tough. It is a way of letting off steam. Play sports, run, jump, compete, swim, or

just bang on a boxing ball. When guys learn to let off steam in non-threatening ways, the family definitely fairs better.

7. Many guys don't drink a lot just to get drunk. It just makes a good place to park their overgrown ego that they don't quite know how to manage well. If he drinks too much and too often, someone needs to find a way to get him to express what's going on inside. Every man needs a good buddy that he can unload on. Absent the mom or a sympathetic ear, there needs to be someone he can express his emotions to about his female problems.

8. Patience is not the average male's best attribute. Stubbornness, on the other hand, comes close to being a typical male feature.

9. Once a guy convinces himself that he is wrong he will usually give up on his own accord, but usually not one second before.

10. There is something about females that men are addicted to. Just as most females love roses or chocolate, guys love sex. That don't mean that you have to have it 24/7.

11. Looking at something that is attractive is not the same thing as having an affair, although some men can't seem to keep their fingers out of the cookie jar. We like fine cars too, but you don't need to sleep in them.

12. Ladies, the things you accuse most men of thinking don't even come close to what he's really thinking. Its hard guys, but you really need to learn to control those wild sexual fantasies.

13. Whoever said that men and boys aren't supposed to cry was off their rocker. We cry, but it is usually in drugs, alcohol, extramarital sex, or other means we don't show you. It would be much cheaper and quicker if society would just let us cry in public without castigating us.

14. When a guy does something wrong it is best to let him know shortly after he did it, rather than in a fight many moons later. We have short-term memory.

15. Many times when we forget things it's an honest mistake. Our brains are not geared to hold on to things that are not in the present moment. Multi-tasking is not our strong suite. We like checking things off the list one item at a time.

16. The average male needs much more sex than the average female. Whatever you are giving your man, try doubling it and that still will not be enough.
17. Women use emotions to draw them into sex while guys use sex to draw them into emotions. Somewhere in the middle the two should meet.
18. You find a lot of females eager to wear the pants in the family, but funny how you don't find that many males as eager to wear the skirts. However, that seems to be changing with the new batch of males.
19. Don't be mad at us because God made us men.
20. Many women would like to see their man tone down the testosterone, but men don't usually have a problem when women turn up the female charm. Of course, that is not accounting for the times when Mother Nature visits.
21. Even though relationships should not be battlegrounds, many of them are made so. Both parties need to be more conscious of their words, deeds, and actions.
22. After the honeymoon period is over, both parties began to draw their boundary lines and defend them with anything necessary to win. The more each party fights for their individuality, the more the couple (team) suffers. Being in a relationship means doing what's best for the union, not for the individual. Human nature compels us to revert back to the self and not to others.
23. In relationships we must learn to control, and many times, overcome our basic human nature.
24. Your body is not something that you can reconstruct (fix) after you have totally messed it up. Guys need to learn to get over this dysfunctional behavior regarding their health.
25. The body is not just a showpiece; it needs to work for a lot of years. If you take proper care of it early, it will take proper care of you when you are older. Take good care of your body; it is the only one you will get on this passage. Go see a professional doctor for regular checkups.

WHAT MOST GUYS NEED TO UNDERSTAND ABOUT FEMALES

1. Females are different from males in many ways. To expect anything to be otherwise is pure ignorance and a time bomb that is only waiting to go off when least expected.
2. Women don't fight using the same battle rules as males. They use whatever advantage they may have that you don't realize.
3. Even though the tongue is one of the smaller members of the human body, it is one of the most effective weapons that females use in the heat of battle. Put on your armor and deflect the flaming arrows that will come in battle.
4. The most important thing a woman needs to feel from her mate is the feeling of security. That is what most females received from their fathers no matter what. Until you make her feel as secure as her father once did, your relationship will not be secure.
5. Guys need to understand the effects of Mother Nature on a female's total self; mind body and spirit. It is like watching a fierce storm approaching from a distance. All you can do is baton down the hatches and wait for the storm to pass over. Waging battles in the midst of the storm is never a winning opportunity.
6. The woman that you courted and fell in love (lust) with during the dating process is not necessarily the same one that you will wake up to shortly after the dust has settled. Get to know your potential mate in ways other than sexually before you commit to saying "I DO!"
7. The ability to please you sexually isn't the most important quality in a woman. If she's a keeper, you need to know what else comes with the package. Take a look at her mother and you may get a hint of your future. (EFJr.)
8. You really cannot make another person happy; that is something they have to do from the inside. However, don't use this knowledge as an excuse not to bend over backwards, or to do every single thing you can think of trying to keep "momma" happy. If "momma" ain't happy, you won't be happy. (CEM)

9. More than anything, a woman wants to be heard. You don't always need to do or fix something about what she is saying, but you do need to take the time to listen to her and make her feel as though you are paying attention. (CEM)

10. Doing small things for no particular reason goes a long way with many women. On the other hand, doing the largest things that you can't even afford is not enough for the other sort. Even if you don't want to, still do nice things for your lady. Keep "momma" happy! (CEM)

11. Men need to understand that no matter what you do, it will NEVER be enough, so if you go in the door with this mindset, it will definitely save you some stress, pain, and heartache!! (EJ)

12. The last thing you want to do with a woman, if you want a successful relationship, is physical intimacy. The most important element in a relationship is establishing a line of communication with one another. Physical intimacy is the lowest form of communication and it is not, I repeat, IS NOT a vehicle to any other form of meaningful communication.(DGC)

13. In order to communicate and understand a woman you must, and I do stress, **MUST** meet and spend time with her family, especially the parents. If you grew up with this person, then you must use this knowledge in learning to understand your woman. Most times, the way the mother relates to the father is the way the daughter will relate to her potential mate or male friend. Environment is a major component in the building blocks of one's character. It should not be discounted. (DGC)

14. Women tend not to forget any wrong that is done to them by a lover or husband. It requires extra effort on the part of the man to reassure the woman that she can trust you again. It is not easy to regain her trust, however it can be done. (DGC)

15. Being right is over-rated…too much compromise on either side is not healthy. (DGC)

16. If a man has to win at the expense or the woman losing, the man loses. (RG)

***This list will be constantly expanded upon at our website: http://realmenseminars.com/ as more men log-in and submit their additions to the short list we have included so far. Please feel free to visit the website and post your comments there to this on-going list. You may also post your initials if you like for other men to see and gain knowledge from your suggestions.

Chapter Four

THE SOCIAL REVOLUTION BETWEEN THE GENDERS

Many people are individually addressing the issues that males are currently experiencing. It appears to be a consensus that something has happened that seriously altered the image, role, and possibly the functions that were previously accepted as the typical image of a man. We have labeled this perception as a *Real Man* just to place a distinction on the subject. Although there is no such thing as a *Real Man*, we are trying to shed light upon something that has shifted in our interpretation of what that role represents. In order to do this, we are focusing upon the body (unit) that is classified as men or males.

Thinking as would a sociologist addressing the subject of "The Shift in Gender Roles of the 21st Century," what would that body of scientific experts share with us? Although several mavericks seem to be addressing this subject individually, it doesn't as of yet appear to have reached an epidemic state. Even though many individuals seem to see a problem rising over the horizon, no one seems to treat is as a major problem. I see it differently. I think if something is not done soon we will see a very sharp reversal of the gender roles as we have known them to exist.

Everything about the statistics shows a dynamic shift in the factors that will eventually lead to this dramatic and drastic shift:

- Women are simply getting better educated and prepared for the job markets while men are slipping down in that area.
- Women are the most reliable member of the family unit while men seem to be disappearing.
- The divorce rate in America is over 50%, leaving the primary care of the children of divorced families in the hands of women.

- Men are choosing to walk away from their families - leaving their parental responsibilities in the hands of the mothers. Mere money does not cut it with children. They also need the contributions of their fathers.
- Equality for females has changed the playing field in the social fabric of society. Women have more choices, more power, more opportunities, and more protection under the law.
- The role of males has been tarnished by the image of heavy handed males unfairly dominating society. Without question, it has been a man's world - with women as secondary partners - since the beginning of historical record.
- The term "male chauvinistic pigs" does have merit and validity. Men operated in that manner as the accepted "norm" of society.
- A shift in laws, enforcements of laws, opportunities, accessibilities, and public perceptions has derailed the stronghold men once had in society.

Although there are a few sharp minds addressing these concerns, they do not appear to be marked URGENT by enough people who have the power to make a difference. If this issue is not addressed urgently, we will have to suffer the consequences of natural evolution that will unfold as the result of the trends that are on the leading edge of society right now. If the current trend continues, women most certainly will take the leadership roles and men will become the secondary partners.

Perhaps it is merely natural evolution that is causing the scale of balance to become equal between the genders. Although equality among the sexes would be the most desired state, especially for females, if males continue to slack in performing their functions they will shift to the lower position in the family structure. It would appear that we may be headed for a reversal of leadership roles.

At this stage it is impossible to determine if such a shift would be better or worse for society because we have never experienced such a drastic change before. Certainly men have had a decided advantage over women since the beginning. If you look at where the male leadership role has taken us as a race (the human race) of people, the picture would not be very pretty. We have become a selfish brood filled with selfish ambitions, warrior mentalities, unequal and unbalanced opportunities, and just overall hard-natured rather than compassionate, caring, and loving to one another. Perhaps it is time for a woman's touch to dominate and bring in some very necessary changes to a picture that certainly could use a gentler approach.

The issue at hand is not the fact that men are not needed in the specific roles they can provide to the family structure. It is more an issue of men losing their focus because of the drastic shift in how women are being elevated, and at times, vindicated as well. Conditions, circumstances, and situations that were unfair to women are being corrected for good reasons. As this male/female dynamic is being changed, it definitely alters how men fit into the unit known as the human race. As shifts are made, it alters both perception and dynamics inside the unit. Remember, there is only so much capacity within a unit. Since we are not creating *new matter* we can only shift the dynamics within the unit. This is what we are witnessing with males today. Using this analogy, we need to figure out how this shift of power is affecting our males. Males will simply need to learn how to make the necessary adjustments and continue to function in this new arena.

KEY MALE ISSUES

This is not a scientific list because quite frankly there is no such thing. It is merely a list of issues that seem to be plaguing many males in this current day society. Some males are affected more than others by certain issues and some not at all. What we are attempting to do is look at a wider body in order to see if we can determine how males appear to be affected as *a unit*. If you were to take your human body and address only the foot, it would not tell you all about the entire body. However, if the foot had a serious gash in it, the whole body would share the suffering. Although males are not connected by a sophisticated network of nerves like the human body, they do comprise a body that is affected as a unit in many ways. The issues cited here are just some of the main ones that seem to be affecting the body of males as a unit.

Through organized meetings and seminars many of these issues are brought up as topics of discussion for male-only group meetings. Amazingly, once men get used to the idea of openly discussing their common issues they sense a common bond. Traditionally, men were not conditioned to speaking openly about things that cause them problems. If it requires admitting that you have a weakness, male pride and ego does not normally allow men to openly confess this. Males are conditioned to *suck it up, be strong, don't show emotions, never let them see you cry,* or just over all *suppress your emotions in public.* Unfortunately, boys learn this at an early age and it remains with them for life.

Psychologically, we are learning that suppressing emotions will cause interior problems within the human psyche. We see it in dysfunctional behaviors and all sorts of addictive dependencies. Men turn to drugs, alcohol, or other crutches in order to squelch the fire that burns inside. They may even turn to extra marital affairs trying to fill a void that they don't understand. Suppressing part of your natural being only leads to a leak in another part of your being. It is as though we only have a limited amount of space inside us that is contained in individual cups. If one cup is filled it spills over into another cup. If all the cups are full they have to overflow the person and spill outwardly. When men cannot handle the pressure, it overflows and turns into dysfunctional behaviors and addictive dependencies.

The following are just a few of the areas where the role of men seems to be drastically affected. Again, this is more a common study than a scientific one.

FATHERHOOD

The role of the father in this current day is not the same as it was during the previous generations. The father <u>was</u> the undisputed head of the household, legally and otherwise. This was supported by law, religion, culture, and public perceptions. Since the father knew his position as the accepted leader he understood that his main function was to lead. Unfortunately, he could only lead from his learned abilities. If he was a weak person, naturally he would not make a good leader. If he had natural weaknesses, that would also affect his ability to lead. If he had a low IQ or intelligence, that would show up in his leadership style. If he had superior skills, intelligence, or talents, that would likewise show up in his leadership abilities. In essence, he was the leader and thereby as the head goes – so would the body.

Since intellectual abilities were never a part of the job qualifications to be the leader, most men led from the hip. They did what they felt should be done in the only way they knew how. Men basically learned to become fathers by watching their fathers or other males. If their father was dysfunctional then unfortunately the male child had that as an example. This does not mean that the child will necessarily be dysfunctional when they grow up, but it certainly means that such traits would be ingrained within their psyche as children that would need to be overcome later in order to resist becoming their father's carbon copy.

Fortunately, there are other factors that go into development of a person that can refute what a *poor father* presented. Mothers always had a dynamic role in their male children. Boys traditionally love their moms and are many times influenced by the mom silently, verbally, emotionally, spiritually, physically, or psychologically. Even a male child with a totally screwed up father may turn out to become a great father, in spite of the influences that may have been working against him.

Without a doubt, children need what both mothers and fathers have to offer by way of parental nurturing. They learn different things from the different gender role models. When children are deprived of either of the roles, a part of their potential would certainly suffer. They may turn out fine, but with quality training from both parents, more behavioral skills are etched into the child's psyche. On the other hand, very poor parental skills from either the father or mother can damage the psyche of a child and become more damning than helpful. For this reason each parent should take their role very reverently.

The main point is, fathers add a potential great dynamic to a developing child and to the family as a unit within society. It is up to individual males to stand firm and become the best role models they can be, not only to their children, but likewise to the human race. A father is something that is very special and very unique. A mother is something that is very special and very unique. Both parties are different and serve a totally different function and purpose. No child deserves to be deprived of a decent father or a mother.

The selection to be born into the world was the result of a male and a female coming together committing an act. The act could have been purely for pleasure or it could have been out of love with the intent to bring a child into the world. Regardless of the intent of the act, the child deserves the best chance to become a fully functioning and healthy human being, capable of carrying on our species. A mother cannot replace a father - nor can a father replace a mother. They are both uniquely purposed to serve a dynamic and necessary human function.

It is important for males to understand what a father adds to the picture and accept that as a divine responsibility. Even though the role may not be the same as it once was thought of, its importance is no less vital than it has ever been. Males must fully accept their roles and responsibilities as fathers. Under no circumstances should children be deprived of what a decent father can add to them. That mission comes from a higher authority than just social pressure. It comes from the very Source of creation itself.

PRIMARY PROVIDERS

Perhaps this role has been singularly altered the most as a result of the recent changes with females. Women are quickly becoming as capable of being the primary provider for the family as males once were. With changes in the laws that forbid discrimination in hiring practices, women are now stepping into jobs that were once male-only positions. Women are now our political leaders, heads of corporations, CEOs, CFOs, airline pilots, business owners, heads of banks, lawyers, judges, astronauts, doctors, chief medical officers, political leaders, and the like. Women command high salaries almost equal to that of their male counterparts for doing the same jobs because of changes in the law. Although things are not totally equal across the board, women are quite capable of becoming the primary financial providers for the family.

Today, women can fill the roles that once were exclusively male. Where does that leave males who may be married or otherwise committed to such females? Are they in competition for the same jobs? Is such competition adversarial or friendly? Can the typical male shallow his pride and allow his female counterpart or partner to assume the lead bread-earner position? The role of the primary provider was the accepted norm for males throughout our entire history. Should this become a cause for major concern as women are assuming that role?

We understand that one of the primary causes of premature death is stress-related. Men developed health issues as the result of high stress that previously did not plague women as much. Men traditionally developed more stress because it was their assumed function to provide for their families. Even though most of the work in the past for males was more physical than it is in today's job market, the necessity to perform any job adds stress, whether it is physical, mental, or emotional. Now that women are stepping into the role of primary providers, studies are showing that they are suffering more stress-related medical issues. There is a cost associated with being the boss. Is that something both parties are willing to accept?

Pertaining to this subject, the main problem with males seems to be with pride, perception, and/or ego, rather than something physical. It is shameful to the average male to think that his spouse is capable of financially outperforming him. Although this is merely an issue of false pride and/or ego, such things can and do affect relationships. Is this a matter of males learning how to swallow their foolish pride and ego, or is that something that men feel intimately threatened over? Were males built emotionally, physically, and spiritually to be in the leadership position or is this something we adopted as a preferred lifestyle?

Regardless of the origin of the roles, the reality is that more and more women are becoming the primary providers for the family. How men deal with the changing of the guard is the issue. Will individual couples sit down and discuss this sensitive subject and agree as to which party will be the primary and the secondary? Or, will this become a continual sore spot between couples? Even though pride and ego tend to place strong psychological pressures upon males, they are not factors that should bring down the family unit. Love and commitment should <u>not</u> be based upon financial potential. Instead, it should be based upon two people coming together as a team and making decisions that are best for the family. Since guys typically love team sports, perhaps they need to consider a committed relationship to be a team affair, rather than an individual failure as it pertains to being the primary bread-earner.

Men need to deal with situations such as this from a *reality basis* and not based upon *what other people think*. Other people do not have to live in your households and/or participate in your family's welfare. A *real man* does what is necessary to accomplish his primary goals. If the goal is for selfish ambitions, pride, and ego over the needs of the family unit, then perhaps he is not good family material. Perhaps he would be better served remaining single and pursuing his personal ambitions, rather than complicating the lives of others just to stroke his mighty ego. Men must learn to put this role in its proper context. Are men there for the team or are they there to please what people think?

CONTROLLING SEXUAL IMPULSES

The desire to have sex seems to be more prominent in males than it does in women. On average, men crave sex much more than women. Since Mother Nature rarely makes mistakes in her design, we must assume this imbalance is for a reason. Perhaps it is because the sense of procreation was placed more in males than females. It could have been a design feature placing the simplest job in males and the more complicated ones in females who actually must endure the entire birthing process.

Of the two genders, females seem to have the more sophisticated design overall while males appear to be quite straightforward and simple. Because of this simplicity, males think only of a simple act of pleasure while females usually involve a more complicated emotional posturing. A female's body has to go through so many changes just to facilitate the birthing ability. With males it is a very simple process. Once the initial union is over the male could disappear. Females do not have that option. Because the role of males during the birthing process can be quite simple, they are more inclined to look merely at the sexual act rather than a more complicated process.

In order for females to become pregnant their bodies have to become fertile even before pregnancy can happen. In addition, the pregnancy process takes time for the embryo to develop. As the females are engaged in the process the male is free to move on to other females and deposit his sperm. Because of this variance in purpose and design, males go straight for the gusto, while females operate much differently in reference to sex.

As part of the natural design females are much more complicated overall than the average male. This is not just physically, but emotionally as well. This complicated design makes them a more stable foundation for the family unit than males. Although many animal species are loyal in partnership, most are not when it comes to procreation. Males are free to roam after dropping their deposits, while females must wait on their reproductive cycles. Perhaps part of our biology makes us as horny frogs. Even so, this does not shape us into the whores we have become in dealing with our sexual addition.

In this day of media influences, it appears that males may be driven psychologically toward sex. It is pumped into our brains and sold as a commodity. Sex, or the implication of sex, is used to lure men into purchasing products. Female sexual features are used to capture the minds and imaginations of males, causing them to be lured toward a particular product. Just as nectar attracts a honey bee, the use of sexual implications attracts the average male. This is not biology, it is psychology. Men must learn how to control and maintain their sexual urges rather than falling for the bait that advertisers use. They exploit a weakness in males, both young and old, in order to sell a product. Are you willing to allow this to happen to you? It's not something that serves you well. You are a simple pun and someone is yanking your chain. If you do not take the controls back in your favor they (the system) will continue to yank your chain and you will be their (B-t-h) sucker. If you don't mind being used in such a manner then keep allowing them to yank your chain.

Although males are naturally attracted to women for obvious reasons, the attraction we see today is not at all natural. We are being influenced by art rather than being the ones doing the influencing. We are attempting to imitate what we see in the movies rather than operating by our natural design. By acting in ways that go against our natural intent, we are creating problems that go against our original purpose. As pleasurable as sex is to the average male, it should not be used in ways that create more problems than good. Sure, it is the reward for people engaged in intimate relationships with each other, but it should not be used like a drink to an alcoholic that can't say no to the next drink. It should not used be like the needle to a heroin addict or the pipe to the crack addict. Instead, it should be used as a controlled substance that one enjoys when it is done, but maintains under will power and self-control when it is over. Part of being human is the ability to make prudent and meaningful choices for the benefit of the species. Are men just as wild as canines, or are they better than that.

Men need to really address their sexual addition. As good as it may be, it is not something that we should allow to control us beyond our own will power. Even if you love chocolates or other fine sweets, it does not mean that you should go out and eat it every time it crosses your mind. We have to learn to exercise more will power and self-control. We need to be in control of the mind and stop allowing the mind to take us anywhere it wishes when the urge comes about.

COMMITMENT

On a related subject, men need to understand the difference between having sex for pure enjoyment sake, versus having it because of a commitment made between two people. Sex is very good between two parties who are on the same wavelength. Both parties give of themselves freely because they want to share their joy with each other. Although there may be a thing called "sport's sex" where both parties just want sexual enjoyment without the commitment, this is not the usual mindset in committed relationships where the parties assume they are each other's one and only sexual partner.

Most people enter into the union of marriage with the expectation that they are the only one privy to the goods. To share that special feature with another party outside the marriage is a breach of trust and a very hurtful thing that one person can do to another. The pain is so unbearable that it could lead to temporary insanity or loss of self-control. Giving freely of one's self with the expectation of commitment is like baring one's soul to another. It is like lowering your defenses and trusting that another person will not hit you in the gut. When one person is deceitful to another it is just plain wrong. If you are a person who would do such a thing to another you should really question your values. If you are willing to stoop that low, and it doesn't matter to you, certainly that says a lot about your character. People of extreme low character are the scum of the earth and not worthy of standing by their fellow humans who have character. If that doesn't matter to you, then continue to do what you do and allow the cards to fall where they may. The universe has a way of balancing the scales of true justice.

With such a harsh statement, I would like to offer an alternative behavior. If a person loves sex with numerous people, and does not want to commit to just one partner, they should make that fact known up front. It is best to be considered an ordinary whore rather than one who lies, cheats, steals, and does other things just to get what they want. Although this may sound a bit old-fashioned, people shouldn't start having sex too soon in the relationship, unless of course, that is the agreement of both parties. As people of freewill, we are free to make such choices, even the choice to kill ourselves, if we wish. That does not mean that there aren't consequences to your actions. It only means you are free to make the choice. Not all things we choose to do are good, nice, honest, noble, decent, right, or helpful. There are times when we do things without the intent to harm others. There are other

33

times when we do things that we know will cause others to suffer. If you are one who does things that you know are harmful and will cause others to suffer you need to check yourself. There is a loose screw somewhere in your moral tool shed that needs addressing.

One of the oldest professions known to mankind is that of prostitution. It is something that mankind has engaged in since as early as records were kept; even long before. Though we may have different personal spiritual convictions, yours are purely your own. We are only bound by the ones we agree to honor. Professional prostitutes provide a service to the people who are willing to pay for it. They don't care if you are married, someone's father or mother, engaged, gay, straight, or other; they only want to be paid for the service they provide. They usually are not in the habit of deceiving anyone other than perhaps stroking one's ego as a part of the service they provide. Would you say that this is an honest profession? Compare this with a married person who has taken a vow of commitment and lies to their spouse and other people who depend upon them as a committed responsible family member. Which party would you consider better or worse? One is honest and one is totally dishonest. You be the judge.

When it comes to making a commitment - taking marriage vows or choosing to become committed partners - people should get to know themselves before they tie the knot. If you are not ready for the big "C" word you should wait until you are. Don't deceive someone who has other intentions if you are not sure. You are free to go out and participate in *wild sex* or *sports sex,* and anything you desire, but do not pull someone else down just to appease your selfish desires. Allow your fellow human beings to remain wholesome and intact while you are going through your experimentation process. Don't pull the rest of the world down just because you are a lowly individual. It is only the right and decent thing to do. Be honest when dealing with others and honest with yourself as well. In doing this you become a *real man.* A *real man* is simply one that exudes high moral character. He does this for himself and, more importantly, for others. If you wish to become real and an authentic person, you will do what is right when the time is right.

ADDICTIONS – DEPENDENCIES – BAD HABITS

Just as people are known to have become addicted to alcohol, tobacco, or other drugs - sex can be an addiction as well. People even become addicted each other. There are people who remain together in spite of all the evidence that says they should be far apart. This is because they are addicted to each other and find it most difficult to make a rational decision. Just as it is difficult to break any habit that has grown to be a dependency, being addicted to a person that you have been with for a period of time can be equally as difficult to break. In order to break most habits it requires a power or force equal to, or greater than, the one you are attached to. You have to pry away the old with a force and replace it with something new in its place.

When you are addicted to a person you may feel that you have to replace one person for another, rather than creating the space to become healthy before you repeat the same mistake with a new person. There are some people who have been married multiple times, and they seem to have the same issues with each marriage. That means that the problem is not with the ex, but with the self. If you are having problems with relationships, find out what is going on in you before you re-engage with another person. This is a topic that is often overlooked when it comes to the subject of addictions.

Besides the usual suspects, there are several other kinds of addictions one must understand. There are also emotional addictions, psychological addictions, spiritual addictions, parental addictions, sexual addictions, pet addictions, sweet addictions, and many more. People are addicted in so many ways to so many different things. In a way we, are all addicted to something in some way or another. Our challenge is to identify our addictions and find a way to break the unwanted habits. We are also aware that there are good habits that we would love to keep. When you decide to get rid of your bad habits, try replacing them with great exercise habits, healthy eating habits, great moral practices, reading habits, study habits, and the like. It is not always the bad things that we can become addicted to. As you are thinking about your possible bad habits, think also of a good one that you may want to use in order to replace the bad ones.

Of the *usual suspects* that become addictions, dependencies, or bad habits, the most common ones that seem to affect most males are drug and alcohol related. These are the most assessable or easiest to acquire. Obviously some drugs are illegal, so becoming addicted to an illegal substance presents a double-edged problem. You not only have the dependency factor to deal with, but also the threat of loss of freedom. If others are depending upon you as a primary provider and you are incarcerated, there is no way to fulfill your responsibility. Many males have succumbed to this beast. The statistics of males serving jail time is alarming and growing. Males are serving jail time at a rate of almost eleven to one over females. Much of this is related to a number of various dependencies.

When people become addicted to substances there is usually a reason behind the addiction. They may drink too much in order to drown certain feelings, inadequacies, faults, unhappiness, rejection, or dissatisfaction with something that is, or is not happening in their lives. The intent is to make the pain or displeasure go away, if even for a temporary moment. Unfortunately, once the effect of the substance wears off, the underline issue remains the same or even becomes more entrenched. This is why it is usually necessary to meet an addiction with an equal or stronger force to oppose it. In essence, you will need a bigger dog to whip the little one you have, even if the little one is a huge ferocious beast.

The typical male has a problem in seeking and obtaining professional help. Men are notorious for <u>not</u> coming forth and dealing with their problems. They don't like admitting they have a problem. That would not be *manly*. On the other hand most men understand that in order to defeat the opposition you need to have a bigger gun than your opponent. Men understand warfare, but not psychology. Even though most people with severe problems could and would be greatly served by using qualified and professional services - that is not something that men do well. You can only lead the horse to the watering hole, but he has to bend down and take a drink on his own, if he's thirsty. You can't teach an old dog (man) a new trick unless that dog wants to learn something new.

If you find yourself immersed in bad habits that you can't seem to break, rather than just applying a band-aid to the problem, why not try to identify the source of the problem and fix it from there? In many cases this requires the services of professionals. An aspirin only makes you forget that you have a pain, but the cause of the pain is still somewhere in your body. When you don't know things, don't be so stubborn as to not ask someone for help. Many strong men die because they choose to be stubborn and stupid. Is your pride worth dying for?

If you have a problem with any sort of addictions, dependencies, or bad habits, become a *real man* by standing up and doing something about your problems. Everyone will love you for making the right choice except for the ones who are addicted with you. They only want a bigger loser than them so they can feel good about themselves. Misery loves company. Losers only hang with their own kind. If you have any addiction problem be a *real man* and put up the best fight you can muster. We already know that until you are ready to change there will be no change happening. Don't wait on fate or the threat of death to get your attention. "Just do the right thing," like Nike ads say, JUST DO IT!

MALE/FEMALE COMMUNICATIONS

Although this topic has been briefly mentioned already, it can't be spoken about too often or too much. One of the biggest misconceptions for men and women, or boys and girls, is to assume that they are more alike than they are different. They are drastically different to the point that they speak different languages, use different methods of measuring and interpreting things, or just processing situations and/or circumstances in an entirely different manner. The problem is not as much in the fact that they are different as it is in their expecting each other to be more alike. The first thing to do is accept the fact that they are drastically different and stop expecting things to be the same.

Women usually respond to things differently than men. Why should that alarm anyone? Men usually do things differently from women. Why does that surprise you? Women are wired differently, made differently, think differently, talk differently, look differently, (thank God), and in all ways, are different. The first rule is to accept the fact that women are different so you can go about learning how to make those differences work to your advantage, rather than being in a constant battle over the most natural phenomenon in the universe. From creation, men and women were designed and intentionally made to be different for specific purposes. Once you understand the nature of intentional design specifications, you may be able to understand why it may be difficult for men and women to communicate. Until both genders accept their differences communication can be very strained.

A huge eye-opener for me was reading the book "Mars versus Venus" by John Gray back in the early 1990s. As I read his book, I could not believe how close he nailed our differences and expectations. Once I understood that as a fact my life totally changed. This was because I no longer expected things to be different than they were. I no longer expected my wife or daughters to be different than their female-like behaviors or responses. Earlier I wanted them to agree with me or understand my point of view, but that never seemed to happen, or it happened less frequently than my patience level could tolerate.

At the same time that I was frustrated out of my wits by being so typically male in my usual behaviors, my wife and other females who had to deal with me felt the same way I did. Since both parties had false expectations, both were equally deceived. Obviously, as I have aged and hopefully become wiser, I have learned to understand and respect these differences. Without the false expectations there is far less stress and more acceptance. It took me so many years to get to this realization. I'm sure many of my gray hairs could have been avoided had I learned this earlier. Most importantly, I could have avoided so much stress by understanding and accepting our differences.

Much of the disagreements couples experience is because of the lack of understanding. The rest, more than likely, can be contributed to our stubbornness, ego, pride, or defiance. Once we understand the differences, communication becomes easier or, at least, more tolerable. Men and women may still disagree over things, but those disagreements would no longer cause World War III once they accept their inherit differences. They simply learn to agree to disagree and let it go. For some, letting it go is the hard part, because they want to win or to have the last word. Even when you win the argument you lose something more precious. You lose peace and harmony, which is worth far more than just a badge saying you were right. You learn to choose harmony over its opposite. You learn to pursue peace over anything else that is analytical or rational.

If you are fortunate enough to make it through all the years of frustration, you even learn to laugh about how silly some of your knock-down, drag-out fights were literally all about nothing. A *real man* eventually learns this secret and can tell the young bulls a thing or two about the art of communicating with (females) women. Just shut up and listen! Don't try to fix anything - just learn to be a good listener.

VIOLENT AND ABUSIVE MALE BEHAVIORS

It is one thing to be an immoral person of bad character that people have to deal with, but a totally different issue when those behaviors become violent and abusive. By the sheer fact that men are physically stronger than females on average, they must exercise restraint when they are involved in heated disagreements or knock-out-drag-down arguments. Although most marital arguments may end up with only harsh, verbal, heated exchanges, many times these disagreements can turn into physically abusive catastrophes. Some people have very deep psychological problems that may be categorized as a sickness. Some have issues controlling fits of rage, anger, or their aggressive tendencies. Some merely snap under pressure and commit atrocious acts of violence. Even though we all have our issues, strengths, or weaknesses, some of them go beyond basic human expectations or what we would consider "rational" behavior.

Violence in relationships is a very serious issue. The inability of two parties to communicate or agree upon things is one of the major contributors. Couples are forced to deal with many things in common, so they must learn to deal with these issues in a way that is not always

39

confrontational. With a lack of communication skills, people resort to other means of attacking each other. When verbal abuse no longer works it may accelerate to more violent measures.

Many people are drawn into battle because they may have control issues. They may have very poor anger management skills, which seems to be more of a personality or behavioral glitch than an illness. Even though people may snap under pressure that does not mean that they are mentally dysfunctional. Most people in relationships have done things that they regret, but those acts were not part of their usual character. When you snap you are in a category of temporary insanity. That means that you are no longer in complete control of your faculties. You would be beside yourself as in looking from another person.

We are the ones responsible for monitoring our behaviors. Temporary insanity is not an excuse for committing violent acts against another person. If the situation happened only one time and never again, perhaps it was only a glitch, but when violence occurs frequently in relationships it is time to make some serious adjustments before it gets out of hand. A friend of mine shared with me something he learned in a domestic violence class. He said, "When shit rises up to your chin, you had better do something before it reaches your mouth." Forgive the graphic language, but it seems to make the point very well.

This may be one of the main reasons why divorce and marital separation are more common today. People are merely deciding to sever the relationship rather than allowing it to accelerate to the next level of violence. If it doesn't fit, don't force it! Walk away! Live to see another day... Do so out of jail.

Because of the physical disparity between the sexes, understandably the law takes sides with females more often than not in disputes and confrontations. Even though it may have been the female that instigated the violence, or even started the fight, the law protects females from the more physically powerful males. Men are also born with subliminal warrior-like behaviors and may be more aggressive when confronted by their mates. This is partly a natural trait and partly a matter of conditioning.

There was a time when boys resorted to dealing with confrontation by fighting rather than by negotiating. Even though women may bark loudly, fighting was not their preferred way of settling disputes. However, with the change in our culture, more women are now resorting to expressing more aggressive behaviors similar to men. With the recent changes in the law and shifts in consciousness, women are more comfortable standing on firm ground rather than backing down in confrontations. Although there is no excuse or rationale for committing violence against another person, in the heat of anger people may revert to their basic animal instincts…This includes both males and females.

On a much deeper level there are other people who are mentally ill. They do not have full control over their behaviors. They are like dry brush that only needs a tiny spark to ignite a major fire. Unfortunately, one does not usually know about this hidden tendency until the spark appears and ignites the fire. By that time, it may be too late because the person may snap and totally lose control. Some of these sick individuals may even have a split personality disorder. Others may learn to cover their skeletons very well.

During recent times we hear of so many seemingly *ordinary people* snapping and committing hideous acts of random violence. Imagine being married to such an individual and learning of it on the evening news? Some are policemen, politicians, firemen, clergymen, or members of the priesthood, neighbors or fellow citizens that we may have previously called our friends. Most of us realize that were there is smoke there is fire, but where there is no smoke - there still could be fire. There is really no way to protect one's self against such acts of violence by sick persons when the warning signs are not visible.

Although this issue is not necessarily a male issue, it does appear to be more common in males than in females. More males are serving longer prison sentences for committing violent acts than females. This is not just a luck-of-the-draw with women getting away with more crimes than men. Men are more violent in nature than their female counterparts. This is part of the male design and part of the feature that makes a male a better protector of the family unit… Men were built for war. That does not mean that men must always exude warrior-like character. When in domestic disagreements men must learn to exercise extreme self-control over their aggressive male energies.

With a planet that is ever-shrinking, more people are forced to live in close contact with each other. With new technology we can see further, move faster, explore deeper, and otherwise get into each other's space more often. We, the people, and especially males, need to learn better ways of settling disputes and disagreements. Our weapons today are far more lethal than just tossing stones or spears at each other. Now we have smart bombs that can be guided by infrared signals from outer space to a tiny dot on the planet. If we do not learn to control our violent and abusive behaviors we certainly will destroy our species. Who wins when everything is destroyed? Similarly, no one wins when people use violence and abusive behavior to cause harm to one another. We must learn to exercise restraint or <u>leave</u>. If you have sicknesses, find a doctor and get the proper help. Just one life is too much to pay for someone's sick violent and abusive behavior. This is not something that is acceptable in any shape or form.

THE RITE OF PASSAGE

One of the major issues plaguing the future of males today is dealing with the "rite of passage phenomenon". We are not properly teaching our boys how to become *real men*. Somehow we have dropped the ball and asked others to fulfill our responsibilities. No man should ever abandon his children or usurp his responsibility as a father. Children need their fathers or someone to stand in the gap on their behalf. If you are a father, that responsibility can only be entrusted to another individual if it is handed off like passing the torch to another runner in a relay race. If a father must leave their children behind for whatever reason, it should be his responsibility to ensure that a strong male is there to take his place. This still does not give him the right to abandon his child. In the older days when a father died it was his brother's responsibility to step in and care for the widow and her children. Somewhere, we lost that connect-ability.

With the understanding that people get divorced, separate as a couple, move away, or anything other than death or incapacitated, a man should never leave the (post) responsibility of rearing his children unattended. You don't necessarily have to be married or living with the child's mother to be a father to them. You don't even need to be in the same household or the same city to be a father to your children. You must make it your responsibility to keep in touch with your children no matter what. Let them know that you are their father and will do the best you can in your absence to be there for them at heart. You must also promise to do your best financially. Even more importantly than mere money, you must show them that you accept and love them. That understanding alone has helped many children keep hope alive until they were strong enough to stand alone without developing deep hidden scars. Children can and do accept the fact that a father may be away from the home, but to be forgotten or ignored is not something that a child can accept, or understand. Even if you can't be there for them physically, make sure that they know you fully accept them as your child. It is in your shadow that they will try to stand, especially the boys, even if it is only in their imagination.

A father means so much to a developing male. His absence goes far deeper than one can count. Even though some boys do quite well in the absence of a father, imagine how much more they could have achieved if they had just known they were loved and accepted by their father.

Individual males may not be able to change the world, but they are capable of changing at least one brick in the wall by insisting upon taking full responsibility for their children. As men raise boys you will notice a direct correlation of strengthening the human race. As men ignore their responsibilities to raise their boys you will see a direct correlation in the weakening of the human race. When we fail our boys, we fail our race. When you father a child, albeit male or female, it is your duty to hold yourself accountable for their fatherhood. Even if you pass the torch to someone else, it is still your responsibility: Once a father – always a responsibility.

Chapter Summation: These are not the only, or the most egregious issues facing our males today. There are merely a few that we know need addressing. Some of this is because of the shift in our customs and culture. Some is because we have problems that have not properly been engaged.

As we look closer and deeper into the social revolution that is currently going on in the world, we need to become more transparent with each other. Where we have sickness we need to address and correct. For years, or even centuries, we knew of certain cancers among us, but we remained silent, knowing wrongs were being committed. We allowed men to abuse women because it was the *silent male code* that said that men were suppose to rule over women. We even allowed people to become slaves to others because it was good for the economy of our nation. We allowed a race of people to be killed almost to extinction in order to take their rich and precious land. At the times when such things were happening people knew it was wrong, but for whatever reason they choose to remain silent.

In this new age we have an opportunity to right a lot of wrongs we know are happening. This is not just a male issue. However, since men assumed the role of leadership they are the ones who need to initiate the change. After all, it was males that led us into this current point in time. If there is a revolution between the sexes, let us put down our guns and pick up our wisdom. Let us do what is right for the family of humanity that we were entrusted to lead.

Chapter Five

THE GREAT DIVIDE

Speaking of revolution, there are many reasons why people are compelled to start a rebellion. When people are abused for too long with no way out, they are forced to fight back for self-preservation purposes. As people are divided into unequal situations or circumstances, they may feel the need to rebel against their oppressors. There are some natural lines of division among people and there are some unnatural divisions. Some differences are part of the natural design and some are merely man's way of carving the world into preferential boundaries. Obviously, he or she who is in power gets the opportunity to do the carving. For centuries the carvers were always males. It appears that this imbalance is currently being adjusted as we live and breathe. Although much of this correction seems to be legitimate and even necessary, we the people must first of all understand what is being corrected, and secondly make our necessary adjustments to the corrections. If we do nothing by way of making necessary adjustments there could be violence or chaos.

Look at what happened when the African slaves were freed by the Emancipation Proclamation that was issued by Abraham Lincoln on January 1, 1863. Although this did not end slavery, it drastically altered the character of the war and transformed the nation as well. Those who were slave owners had to make the adjustments, because shortly afterward it became illegal for a man to own another man as chattel property. Those who were in power did not like the change, but the change was legitimate and necessary. Slowly, the people made the necessary adjustments. These adjustments are still being made today since that law was passed way back in July of 1865, nearly a century and a half ago.

Even more recently women won the right to vote back in the 1920s for our national elections in America. They further gained equality in

1964 with the passage of the civil rights act. When necessary corrections are made people are forced to make their adjustments to the corrections or there could be violence. Change does not usually happen immediately; it has to be filtered into the existing systems.

Unfortunately there are many issues people hold that create division; race and gender are just two of the dividing lines, but there are many more that people seem to hold on to in spite of the fact that they do not serve the greater good. In essence, we have many dysfunctional behaviors in human kind. If you honestly look at many of these behaviors no one in their right mind could say that they are good for all the people. What good does it serve to keep a group of people down just so another group can prosper? We all lose as a race of people.

What is served when we judge others by our standards, rather than allowing them to elect how they wish to live, even when their system conflicts with our own? Obviously when systems counteract each other it becomes a natural conflict that has to be resolved by some measure. However, just because someone chooses to do things differently, as long as it does not affect your freedom or privacy, that shouldn't become a major issue. When it does affect you personally, division lines are created that could cause violence and chaos. Unfortunately, we have not evolved enough in consciousness that we handle our differences well.

This subject involves more than just the minor differences between people, such as gender, but it also involves our basic composition. Like a prairie filled with assorted wildflowers, we come in all sizes, shapes, colors, genders, preferences, cultures, nationalities, persuasions, and other distinguishing qualities. If we have a bone to pick with others just because they may be naturally different, it is not the difference that is the problem; it is instead the person's mindset that usually makes it an issue. Ironically, most of the conflict over the issues does not involve the natural element, but instead unnatural human behaviors. Prejudice, bigotry, bias, ridicule, meanness, belittlement, ostracizing, and the like, are not natural elements. They are merely the flavoring we add to the natural elements that are instigated by human nature.

If we were somehow able to stick to the natural elements that caused the differences, perhaps we could learn to value and even appreciate the great smorgasbord of humanity. Each difference actually adds a particular quality and a choice that we may enjoy. What one sect does not have can be provided by another? What skill may be missing in one flourishes in another? If we look for benefit rather than criticism we would all be better served. For some strange reason, we feel more threatened by our differences than excited about what they may offer. This attitude is not based upon something natural; instead it is based upon a flaw that exists within our ordinary human nature.

In order to correct this problem that we have allowed to become an ocean that divides us, we only need to step back and separate the natural from the unnatural. Going against nature, or what is natural, creates conflict, while going with the natural flow of creation usually creates harmony. Swimming upstream is going against the grain and much harder than swimming with the natural flow. Even though we don't expect life to be totally easy, we can make it better when we learn to see the purpose of life and work with it rather than against it. Obviously, this does not apply in all cases, but for the most part the universe was built on natural elements that cohesively work together in harmony. We are the ones who create the great walls of divide.

GENDER WARS

One of the greatest oxymorons is a war between the sexes. Another one is that of religious wars. Men and women were made for each other. To start a war between two things that were made for each other has no rationale. Although our differences may rub us harshly, we need to work more on understanding our differences rather than using them to make war. Similarly, a religious war over God seems to be idiotic. No matter what someone worships as their god, unless they believe that gods are adversarial beings who love to see their servants in constant battle, there is no basis to fight over who one claims to be the Ruler and Maker of the universe. Even if someone believed that the one we know as the devil was the creator of the universe, and the one we call Lord God Creator is merely a lower servant of the devil god - that still would not be a reason to wage a religious war. If anyone's god is as strong and powerful as their believers claim, he or she (their god) would not need petty, mortal human beings waging battle in order to defend him or her. Gender wars are about as ironic as religious wars, but that is only an opinion. To each their own opinion…You know what they say about opinions?

Although most of us have heard the statement, "Make love not war," if we did not learn to make love rather than war this planet would quickly come to a screeching halt. Can you imagine women suiting up for battle against men? Of course they would have to make themselves all pretty for battle because they would be in the presence of their male nemesis. They couldn't miss the opportunity to impress their potential captives and prove that they were the superior gender. If women did not have what they have - they would not have power over males. Men freely admit that they are addicted to women, so what is the big fuss that is worth fighting over? On the other hand women probably think that men can't get along without them? TRUE! They probably also think that men would run this planet into the ground without women? Also TRUE?

No matter what women say, most men would probably eventually agree with them, because it is a fact, we can't, nor do we wish to even consider the remotest possibility of even attempting to get along without them. We rest our case and the women can win the war. We surrender! Let that be the end of the war! Now can we just make love…

MASSIVE CORRECTIONS

While we are in the mood for love and for change, why don't we make a few more beneficial changes for the benefit of our species and our planet? Revolutions don't come along every century, so while we have the doors open we might as well throw out the old dysfunctional baby with the stale bathwater. We tend to hold onto things even when they aren't working, simply because that was the only thing we knew. Slowly and surely, we seem to be evolving as a species. Once upon a time, we were literally afraid of each other for no reason other than fear or ignorance. Now that we have gotten to know one another better, we can at least get rid of the ignorance that separated us. People are not naturally born with hate in them. They learn to hate based upon prejudices that are taught. As you see little children playing with one another, they do not see differences unless someone points them out. They only see someone that looks similar to them that may present an opportunity to share some fun with. Even if they saw differences they would not make it an insurmountable barrier. While we are open to change, why not go all the way and start doing things just because they are the right things to do? Don't do things based upon what others may say, but based upon a gut feeling of doing something nice for someone. You know when your intent is to be nice or to be naughty.

BIRDS OF A FEATHER

It is true; birds of a feather tend to flock together. There is more familiarity between them, which makes it easier for them to communicate and understand each other. This is not intended to offend any other birds, but to make it easier to carry on with life. As you look at most of the animal kingdom, most like or similar animals tend to hang together. You don't see elephants trying to hang with the giraffes or the tigers hanging out with the baboons. Each species shares a common bond and likeness so it makes it easier for them to live their lives and carry out their purposes. The walls that are created by this natural grouping were not intended to tear down something, but rather to build up and protect something. When you look at the rest of the inhabitants of our planet, you can see how nature designed things in a natural manner in order to achieve specific purposes.

If we look at our race, we see many similarities in the nature of being warm blooded animals. We tend to group in flocks by similarities when possible and communicate easily and freely with those of which we have the most in common. People that speak the same language and understand the invisible nuances tend to gather naturally with each other in order to make their lives easier. Imagine being in a neighborhood where you are the only one who speaks your language. Wouldn't that make it a bit harder to get along with your neighbors? Some of our groupings are just part of natural selection or convenience and are not intended to be taken negatively. When people take natural things and turn them into negative perceptions – that is where the problem lies.

We know that certain animals mark their territory with urine or other markings. We know that certain animals have predatory instincts. Are we to think that we are the same as the lower animals? Weren't we given abilities that are notably superior to the lower animals? We were born Homo sapiens. We were not born baboons, lions, or apes. Our behaviors should not be like the lower animals even though we are ourselves an animal type. The things that separate us from the lower animals are our power to think rationally, to make analytical choices, to use reasoning, to be compassionate, and to use our brains in ways that no other animal can. If we wish to live and act as the lower animal, perhaps we want to go out into the wild and hang with the beast of that likeness. As human beings we are expected to act and be more than just a dumb animal that only follows his instincts. My fellow humans, we are more than that!

As men it is important for us to recognize our differences, but not to allow them to create great walls of divide between us. We don't need to mark our territory or fight to the death in order to acquire the best females. Although we have our boundaries, many of them are useful because different tribes or groupings of people honor certain laws and rules that have become the custom of their people. We have protected borders around our country because we have an agreed upon set of laws that are unique to us, while others may not respect the same laws. It would be nice if there were sameness in the laws, but that is not the case and never will be because birds of a flock tend to flock together.

Usually, there is commonness or even a strong bond among African American males that is different from that of pure Africans or Pure Americans. The same could be said for Hispanics from different parts of the globe: likewise Asians, Persians, Caucasians, Greeks, Jews, Indians, and the entire gamut. When you look at just race, there are actually only about 5 races of people in the world, but many ethnicities and variations from the root races. They are said to be: Mongoloid, Caucasoid, Australoid, Negroid, and Capoid. This theory, originally proposed by Ashley Montague, has been widely disputed for years. Regardless to the divisions, we can see how all races share about 99.99% of the same genetic materials. One thing we know for sure is that we are not bound by any such differences as a measure that should keep us at bay from each other. It is merely how birds of a feather tend to find comfort with each other.

As you began to learn more about the different races and cultures, it usually adds an appreciation of how people developed in unique ways over time and history. It is interesting to see how certain gifts, talents, and likenesses have been modified in certain people. Even though most of those cultural differences are unique and interesting, when you separate males from females, it usually draws back to commonness. Except for strict cultural differences, the male/female dynamic seems to be one of our most clearly cut lines. Men are men and women are different. I'm sure they would say the opposite. Women are women and men are different. Awe!

Chapter Conclusion: In essence this great divide is something that we created, and likewise, it is something that we are totally empowered to eradicate. As we began to understand our differences and accept the fact that differences are part of the natural design, then we can move on to appreciating, or at minimum, respecting such differences. There is no need to construct great walls to strictly keep others out, other than when used to enforce respect of each other's agreed upon laws. We are not like the lower animals that only know how to be one way and that is the way they were born to be. We on the other hand have choice. We are supposed to have intelligence, reasoning, and the ability to negotiate or compromise with each other. If there is war we choose to go to war. It is not something that we have to do, but something we merely choose to do. It should be our goal to find ways to tear down the walls and open our doors to share with one another what we so uniquely have to offer. We only have one world that we must share. It would be nice if we would willingly share it with each other in the name of brotherly love and peace.

If men truly want to run the world as respected leaders, they will have to learn to tone down the aggression and learn to get along with each other in spite of all the differences. A *real man* is one that understands that all men are our brothers, even though they may be of a different mother. We all were born of our mothers. We all developed in her belly and came out as human being, Homo sapiens, and males. When you learn to see the bigger picture the smaller things cease to be a problem.

Chapter Six

KNOWING YOUR ROOTS

If we could take a peek back in time close to the very beginning of human life on this planet, I wonder, what we would see? Much of this would depend upon which camp you subscribe to regarding the actual beginning; evolution verses creation. Although I have my own religious convictions and/or perceptions, what I believe to be true only affects me, not the actual truth of what really was. Scientifically speaking, we know that either there was one couple that everyone originated from, or at minimum, only a few early human beings that seeded our entire population. No matter which way you believe it started, there is still a long history we have on this planet. We have a foundation upon which our species was built. This foundation was our roots. There is much to learn from knowing something about your roots.

I can imagine during our earlier days we were very much uneducated in terms of what we would consider to be formal education. Obviously, there were no books to teach from simply because things such as written language had not been created in the beginning. For eons of time people could neither read nor write. People from various areas of the planet spoke different languages and developed according to the geography they lived in. For example, humans who lived in cold weather climates experienced life quite differently than those who lived in tropical areas. Their diets, manner of gathering food, customs, shelter, clothing, and so many different things about their development were necessitated by the weather and the geography. Even the way such people looked was influenced by the weather, in addition to the entire environment in which they lived.

We can imagine people with dark skin came from places that were closer to the equator, while people of light or white skin came from places that had not as much exposure to sunshine year around. We can imagine that people who grew up inland away from large bodies of water developed much differently from those who lived around major water ways. We know that certain plants and animals are indigenous to certain geographical areas of the planet. Further, we know that people who lived among and nurtured from these different plant and animal life would have developed quite differently. If you look at people who are vegetarians, compared to people who eat meat, you will notice substantial differences between them. Imagine how much a hundred or even thousands of years of developing in one way or another would alter how different people eventually developed?

One thing we can't dispute is the fact that we are made up of 99.99% of the same genetic material. In spite of all the differences in the ways and elements that we developed, you would imagine that there might be more differences in us than just that .01%. What that tells us is that perhaps at one point all of mankind originated from the same source. Who knows how many years it took to evolve just that small percent of differences? It also tells us that something about our genetic or DNA structures gave us our design structure besides the relatively small exterior differences. You might wonder how something so sophisticated could have just showed up thousands or even millions of years ago. Just the genetic and the DNA structure alone is one of the most sophisticated of all known structures. Such intelligence appeared long before we even knew how to speak, write or even communicate with each other.

This makes one wonder, where does intelligence come from? Is it something that made itself or was it made? This is an interesting question, because in order to understand our very own being we would have to ask the same question. Did we evolve into beings that already had the most sophisticated compositions or did something create us? Perhaps this sort of questioning leads to what we know as religion, but religion is merely our method of coming up with answers to questions we cannot answer. The substance that makes up our religion is the real thing, not what we think it may be. DNA is real. Genes and cell reproduction is real. Photosynthesis, animal and human reproduction abilities, and a host of things that comprise life, are real and they are already here before our very eyes. How it all got here is still a mystery to us. Sure we have our theories and speculations, but no matter what we think or speculate, we cannot dispute the fact that all this very complicated and sophisticated stuff is here. And, it works in ways we may never totally understand.

We have already mentioned the term "human nature" a few times in this material. Human nature quite simply is just the ordinary way we do, act, think, or operate in given situations or circumstances. Some of this is learned and some of it comes naturally. No one has to teach us how to breathe, but someone does need to teach us how to speak. No one has to teach us how to walk, but they may have to help us stand up for the first time. No one teaches our hair to grow, eyes to see, nose to smell, ears to hear, heart to pump blood, and a host of things that we do automatically, because it is born in our nature or, natural being.

However, as I have also mentioned before, many things that we have become were not part of our natural being. Perhaps a slight part of our personality comes through our genes, but the majority of it comes from our immediate environment. We define our personalities as the measurement of our traits, which is further defined as our habitual patterns of behavior, thought, and emotions. In essence, what we come to know as a person is the collection of their trait patterns, not the blood, flesh, bones, hair, DNA, genes, and the like. We actually relate to each other from what we exude outwardly rather than what we are inwardly. If what we perceive about each other comes mainly from what our environments make us into, rather than what we really are inwardly, what does that say about life in general? It says that life is pretty much what we make of it.

As human beings we are more sophisticated than we will ever know, but that is not as much the issue as it is what we do, how we behave, the things we say and do, and yes, also how we perceive things. Our perceptions dictate how we operate within the knowledge we think we know and believe. If I truly think of a person as my enemy I would definitely treat them differently than if I perceived them to be my friend. How many of your relatives or friends were once very close to your heart until they did something to break the bond of trust, then all of a sudden they became the vile of the earth. Their DNA or genes did not change. What they physically were as a person did not change, but their façade changed in your mind so they became a negative thing rather than a positive. (This does not happen as frequently with males as it does with females.)

Although such things become part of our human nature they are not real. The real is the same person that was once your friend and now is not your friend. The human being is still the same. Since only the façade changed rather than the real, we should learn to place less stock in the façade and more in the real. The one distinction that separates us the most from the rest of the animal kingdom is the fact that we have the ability to choose what we think and perceive. Even when people do you wrong or offend you there is still a personal choice you may make. You can hate them for what they did or you can forgive them and continue relating to them. Even though that person may have made a mistake… that may not be what that person really was inwardly.

At the same time, we also find that people we thought we knew and loved revealed a part of their character that you never imagined. From that knowledge you may choose <u>not</u> to be friends or even associate with such a person. There is something about getting to know people from their roots that could make all the difference in the world.

Although this premise was longer than I originally intended I want to use it to speak primarily about our distinction of males and females. Part of what we see is a façade and part of it is anatomy. Part of it is biology, part chemistry, part personality, and part just ordinary human nature. As you are attempting to understand people in general there are a lot of distinctions to weigh, but why not instead look at the obvious.

In judging people, look at their character as well as how they look physically. Character can be faked for a short while, but people can't practice being nice for a long time if it is not in their character. Eventually, they would slip and allow the real deal to become exposed. If you look at the male/female dynamic from this prospective, perhaps you will see an entirely different picture than just looking at the obvious physical appearance. Take a look behind the curtains.

THE CHARACTER OF A MAN

The character of a man or woman is what is in their heart. First of all, we need to distinguish the difference between what comes out of the mind rather than the heart. Our minds can be very tricky and even deceitful, but usually our hearts don't lie. What is in the heart usually comes out of it. When a person is sincere, serious, kind, courteous, compassionate, loving, trustworthy, thoughtful, considerate, or even-tempered, this is stored in their heart. Such persons will act and react a certain way because that is what they are. They do not have to manufacture or pretend to be these things. It is their nature. These are the things that make the character of a man. Much of this is learned behavior, but some may be born into people who seem to have a predetermined nature about them. Take the above list of characteristics and see if you can come up with their opposites. Those characteristics are likewise learned behaviors.

People are not "stuck on stupid." Just as they learned their poor character, they can change if the desire is there. People don't tend to change until they are ready. You see this in children. Even though they are not as powerful as adults you may see them stand up and defy the much larger and more powerful adult. This may be a defiant nature, but it is usually because the parent allows the child to act that way without strong opposition. People may think they are being nice to their children by letting them do whatever they like, but that is not being nice; instead it is shaping their character to become something very un-nice. Since character is developed, it is quite necessary for parents to stand guardian over their children and iron out poor character as they see it develop. If poor character is not met with strong resistance it develops into a habit, and further becomes the personality.

By merely looking at some young men or boys you can almost see their upbringing by the way they behave. Some parents will say that they did the best they could under the circumstances, but that would not be entirely true. The character of the person reveals what was or was not done. If the outpouring of poor character was not met with strong resistance early on, it created the bad character that we see later on. We see this situation a lot with single women raising defiant boys. No reflection on the mom, but if they don't have the power to enforce strong boundaries the boys (or girls) will become whatever is most natural to them. Just as water always takes the path of least resistance, children will do the same. During my childhood a hard head made for a soft behind. For some reason modern day parents are reluctant to discipline their children with ample enough force in order to ensure their character is shaped properly.

The character of a man starts by shaping him as a child. If they are allowed to get away with things that go against the basic rules of conduct it will surface in their adult character. People may ask, what are the basic rules of conduct? Although many tend to use a sliding scale, there are some that no one can deny, if they use common sense. Disobedience goes against the basic rules of conduct. If children disobey a direct command from the parent it must be met with strong opposition. You can only send the child to their room so many times, or tell them to take a "time out" so many times, until the child adjusts to the punishment or turns it into something they like. Meanwhile, they continue to disobey because they know the punishment is "no big deal." On the other hand, if a child gets a spanking or some strong force when they disobey a direct command, they will think twice before they disobey the next time.

One of the best human deterrents is the threat of pain or loss. Although I do not advocate cruelty to children, if they are not disciplined the alternative may be far worse than a sore behind and a few tears. Even with this stated, some people are flatly against corporal punishment with their children. That is a choice they are free to make, but they should also weigh the consequences both ways. Do we want to aid our children in building good character or do we want them to be happy while they are young and grow up to be something not so nice? Later on we will speak more about parenting, however, it is important to understand that well developed boys are the ones who grow up to become well developed men.

TURN BACK THE HANDS OF TIME

Physically we know we can't turn back the hands of time, because once something is done it can't be undone. We can do it again differently, but we can't undo what was done in the past. One second ago was and is in the past. The fact that a person may have had a bad childhood does shape the character of a man, but many men, thanks to the support of friend and loved ones, make the choice to turn their lives around.

I once knew a kid who was very mean, angry, defiant, disobedient, rude, and an all around rotten kid. He lost both his mom and his dad and had to stay with an aging grandmother. He was fortunate to have other caring relatives because many kids end up in foster homes where they become wards of the state. This is no dark reflection on foster homes, but certainly loving parents or relatives offer children more than most foster homes can provide. However, even with that stated, we cannot always control how life unfolds. This kid I mentioned got a bad draw from life and that affected his character and his life. It was not the kid's choice to lose his parents. Life happens!

Strangely, after a few years passed by not seeing this kid, later I saw him slightly older. He had made a drastic turnaround. He joined the cub scouts where a scout leader took an interest in him and helped him turn his life around. The kid developed goals and had something that he wanted to achieve, rather than accept the cards had been dealt to him. We are not forced to keep the cards we draw from life. Things can change, but it usually does not happen by osmosis. Change requires replacing the bad with something that is good. If a kid has nothing and cannot see a future, he has nothing to look forward to. Once someone helps him dream or teach him that good things are possible, they may want to change their own circumstances in order to get the things that dreams are made from. Fortunately, this kid made a substantial change in his life even before he became an adult. Imagine what kind of man he would have become had his life remained on the same track? We have too many of our boys on the wrong path and no one is pulling them to the side and giving them better options. We must change this if we want to preserve the brotherhood of men. We have to take our boys and help them become men of character.

Even though our roots may help shape us into the men we become, we can always become better men of sound character if we desire to do so. We may not become financially rich or famous, but it doesn't take luck or finances in order to develop good character. Even if you are the worse of the worst, you can rise to become the best of the best.

I haven't read George W's biography yet, but from what I heard, he was not the model man during his early adulthood. He went on to become the President of the Unites States of America. I read some of the early years of Barack Obama. Apparently he did not have a very cultured or sheltered childhood either. His father left the family early in his development. This scarred him I'm sure, but he did not accept that as his final determinant. He went on to become a Harvard Law professor, a US Senator and on to the next president after George W.

We are not forced to remain in lower positions no matter what the odds or the circumstances. With the proper assistance we can reshape and rebuild our lives. We start the process by rebuilding our character. If you know you have poor character, just make the choice to change it and your entire life will have improved. It does not take money to establish the worth of a man; it takes character. A poor man can be rich in character. A rich man can be a damn fool. Character cannot be purchased, but certainly money can buy many foolish things. The measure of a man is his character.

THE SIGNIFICANCE OF OUR ROOTS

In this chapter alone we spoke about things back in the beginning and how various factors became the building blocks of the people we eventually became. Knowing something about your roots may assist you in understanding things about people in general. Apparently, things happened for a reason and those reasons made things into what we see now. We know that we have animal tendencies within us, so it is important to learn how to control parts of your nature and not allow things to go anywhere they want to go. When we see certain traits in ourselves that are undesirable we have the ability to change them if we so desire. I would like to speak a bit deeper about the significance of our roots, because it may likewise help us see a broader picture of humanity.

In this analogy, let us use root in the manner of a seed. A seed carries all the information in order to produce most of our plant life and vegetables. Imagine a tiny seed that turns into a giant sequoia tree. Everything about that huge tree is contained in its tiny seed. The size the tree will become, its root structure, leaf design, bark design, color, seasonal patterns, watering system, nurturing manner, and the like is in that seed. It is incredible how a tiny seed can tell everything that a plant needs in order to carry out its entire life and function. Another example is that of a watermelon or fruit seed. If you plant it in California soil it will produce watermelons. If you plant it in Florida soil it will still produce watermelons. The same would be true if you planted it in Australia, New Zealand, New York, Paris France, London England, or soil anywhere in the world. A watermelon seed will always produce a watermelon. How does a tiny seed know how to do that? Where is that signal of pure intelligence coming from?

At the root origin, or the seed, are contained all the instructions that everything will become including the purpose it should serve while it lives. Likewise, the moment a sperm and an egg come together and form an embryo all the instructions for that being is already in place. Where is all that intelligence coming from? If we could extract just the intelligence from a seed or an embryo, its knowledge would fill several books.

Although there are many factors that make us into the men we become, some of them are far beyond our ability to control. But, certainly there are many that are within our grasp. If we truly want become better, more reliable and dependable men… that is certainly an option we may choose. In order to become a real (authentic) man it has to be done first with a conscious choice. Yes, your roots may be a factor, but your choices can override many obstacles as well.

Perhaps this goes under the category of "tell me something I don't know," but I find it quite interesting when we look into where we come from and how all that happens. Since most men are analytically minded, this at least makes good food for thought. I'm not sure if this makes a case for a Creator or not but you sure have to wonder where all this intelligence comes from. Sometimes, only asking the questions will prompt receiving an answer.

Regardless of all the scientific and technical stuff, one thing is for certain; we are already here in the pool. We may choose to swim or sink. You are the one that makes the difference. At the end of the day all you need ask yourself, "Is my life made better or worse because of what I know or don't know?" If knowing your roots helps make you a better man, then I would say, get to studying. Seek and you will find. Better still, become a seeker and what you are seeking will be attracted to the energy that you emit. It all starts at the root of your being.

Chapter Seven

THE ROLE OF MEN TODAY

If you were in a rut, understanding how you got there may be of assistance, but dwelling on how you got there will not in itself alter your situation. You actually need a tool, a method, a step, or some sort of plan that you might initiate in order to get you from your current point (the rut) to the point you are trying to reach, which is out of the rut. So far, we spent a lot of time talking about the past, which is the root of the situation. But, just dwelling on the past will not improve where we stand right now. If you did not plan for success, chances are you are not currently experiencing it. Not a problem; start planning right now! If you prepare and follow a decent plan it should lead you on a path of success.

The life you are facing today is not the life your father saw. The life he saw was very different from yours. How things worked in your father's hay-day are much different now. Likewise, our children will see a world much different from the one we are experiencing. The bottom line is, the past is gone and the future will never be present. All we really have is the current moment to start doing things in order to make our lives better now, if that is our heart's desire.

We have already documented the changes in the lives of females. As their lives changed, naturally ours did also because we share lives together. You are looking at a team when dealing with relationships. If one member of the team changes it alters the entire team. There's no question that the role of women today has drastically changed over the past few decades. Women are not just stay-at-home housewives. It is quite common for women to work in the workplace nearly as much as men. Since there are many women serving as the heads of a household, they are forced to assume the role of both homemakers and financial providers. When married or committed females spend a great deal of time in the workplace, the dynamic of the family unit has to change. When the dynamic of the team shifts, everything shifts.

The way change affects society nearly always come in stages. First, the actual threshold of change passes through in streams of consciousness. Next the hearts and minds of people gradually become accustomed to the new changes that already passed. With some changes people catch on slowly and some they are forced to accept immediately. Necessity is the *mother of invention* and *the big dog that must be fed.* For example, when bills are not paid there are severe consequences. If you do not have money you can't provide the necessary things one needs just to survive. Necessity will require that something must be done in order to eat, cloth yourself, and to find shelter. If there are no resources people become homeless and depend upon begging, handouts, or public assistance programs. In bad economic times more families find themselves out of resources and very much down and out. Even when the economy starts getting better, the threshold of change slowly filters through society. In essence, change is rarely immediate when it comes to public awareness and perception. It takes a lagging process before is filters throughout.

Currently, the role of males in society is experiencing this lagging process of change. The threshold has already passed through, but it has not completely filtered throughout the people. If you look at the racial and gender revolutions of the 1960's and 1970's - to the changes in technology from the 1980's and 1990's, so much changed in a short time, but the people still have not completely adjusted to those changes.

With the changes in the civil rights laws, women started competing for the same jobs as men. Minorities who were once blocked or restricted from certain advances in the job markets were aided by stricter enforcement of the civil rights laws. This created new hiring practices. These changes directly affected the families who had depended upon the status quo all their lives. We went from typical family styles like "Ozzie and Harriet" to "All In the Family," to "The Jeffersons," to "the Cosby Family," to a host of inter-racial, cross gender, and nearly "anything goes" styles as a society. All these changes happened before the will of the people accepted them. Even to this day, our senior citizens have a hard time trying to totally grasp the totality of such drastic change. Quite naturally, the role of men in society has to change in order to reflect all these social revolutions. Like the game of musical chairs, all the members will have to jockey for their new positions.

Right about the same time, or just behind the racial and gender revolution, technology created major changes in how labor was performed. Instead of the more common and numerous manual labor jobs, the new era required more technical training. Factories, mills, and entire industries were no longer operating in the same manner. Agriculture was no longer one of the top job markets. Factory jobs began thinning out. Even many assemble line jobs are being phased out by industrial computers that can do many times the work of humans and much faster, efficiently, and do so at a fraction of the cost. In addition, many industries are shipping their job orders overseas where the labor is cheaper.

This drastic and radical change hit males much harder than females, because most of those common labor jobs were held by men as a carry-over from the male-dominated days of the past. Today we are seeing a gradual shift in the workplace of more women and less men. When the dust finally settles, one can only speculate upon where men will stand in the total job market. Will men still maintain their advantage in the amount of jobs held? If women outnumber men in the workplace what will that do to the family structure? One thing is already certain; the role of men in current day has changed from what it was just a short while ago.

THE CURRENT PERCEPTION

Although the facts are probably not as dismal as it appears regarding the image of men today, if the current trend continues women will certainly outnumber men in the workplace in the near future. On average, they are becoming better educated, better trained, and better prepared for the job markets than males. Certainly this will translate into females becoming better employed, because they will be better suited for the jobs at hand. In addition, men die younger, more men are incarcerated, and more men are unavailable for heterosexual relationships with females. Certainly the gay-factor does have an influence upon the male/female dynamic. The perceptions do not look very promising. If things continue on the current trend a major change is just around the bend. Is this our destiny?

There is a perception that boys are not learning to become strong men as once was the case. This is mainly because so many men are no longer teaching their boys how to become strong men. One of the reasons is because the world no longer reflects what older men know. If a man only knew common ordinary labor skills and those jobs are no longer available, what can he teach to his son with authority? If older men do not understand modern technology, they feel somewhat out of place and inadequate as a good teacher. Although acquiring a good paying job is a very important role to most males, it is not the total measure of a man. As we have mentioned, the real measure of a man is more in his character. If his character is very sound he will make prudent decisions regarding how to properly manage his life. If a man is of poor character then no amount of education or job skills will make him a total success in whatever he decides to do. The one thing that a father can teach his son is good character. If the older man is not of good character, he has very little to offer his son that will assist him in truly succeeding in life. This is something that men will have to assume as a responsibility.

TEACH THEM TO FISH

If you give a person a fish sandwich they may still go hungry after a short while, but if you teach them how to fish then they can catch their own fish and make their own fish sandwiches. Even if a father cannot teach his son technical job skills, he can teach them things such as good work habits. He can teach them honesty and fair dealing. He can teach them integrity and being a man of his word. He can teach them the importance of being punctual, tidy, and ready to take advantage of opportunities once they come his way. A person with good traits, character, and mannerisms can compete well in certain job markets because they are deemed to be more dependable and reliable.

If a person is not trustworthy, no one in their right mind would want to hire them and trust them to do what is best for their company.

Even though the father may not be the one who actually does the teaching, his function is also to provide the best opportunity he can for his children. He may not be able to send them to the best colleges or universities, but he can be a great father and guardian, making sure they do well in school and exemplify good behavior both at home and in public. How we guardian our children could make all the difference in the world. We need to teach them decent morals and values so as they mature that will exemplify who they become. Many parents did not earn higher education degrees, but made it very important that their children take advantage of opportunities that were not available when they were growing up. We lead by example. We become role models for our children and guide them toward opportunities that we may have missed ourselves. What a parent offers to their children is not always measured in finances or intellectuality. We can teach our boys how to become strong and reliable men of good character and to be the best they can with what they have to deal with. We teach them how to fish and trust them to fix their own sandwiches.

RE-EVALUATE AND RE-EDUCATE

Many men over the age of fifty may feel that they have missed a major learning curve. Many of them are intimidated by technology. On the other hand, most young people in general grew up with technology. To them there was never a time without computers, cell phones, social networking capabilities, text messaging, emailing, and the like. The reason young people pick up new things better is because they are not afraid of technology. They are instead eager to learn and experience new things. Perhaps dealing with older men has something to do with teaching older dogs new tricks?

The capabilities we have today far exceed what many older people are willing to venture into. It is as though they are afraid they will break something. People tend to avoid things they fear. The worse part of fear is fear itself, or not knowing what to expect. Once you get over the fear… learning becomes much easier. Because of this, most of us need to re-evaluate our fears and educate ourselves to this modern technology.

In order for us to progress as a gender, the normal process had always been from the older to the young, which usually translated to the mature to the immature. However, when it comes to learning new technology, older people can learn much from the children. Don't be too proud to ask your children how to use certain features on the more sophisticated cell phones or computer programs. Even if they don't know they are not afraid to try. You, (older men) on the other hand, are too proud and too afraid to admit that you have a problem. If we are to turn this declining image of males around, we need to re-evaluate the pride factor and re-educate ourselves to the changes of the 21st Century.

YOU ARE YOUR AGE

You may have heard that age is a state of mind. To a certain extent that may be true, but you are the age you are. With that come certain realities. We were born for the age of which we live and serve humanity. If you were born in the 1920s' that time slot marked the start of your designated time here on earth. Those who were born in the era of the baby boomers, after World War II, certainly came at a different time in history. At the same time, those who were born in the new 21st century will have their own time and space. It is the nature of time and change: "To each their own and a time for all things." We cannot live the lives for our children. All we can do is teach them as best we can and trust them to bring in their generation and do the best they can likewise.

We should not live in regret of what is coming or what was not to be. As we are alive we have the opportunity to make a difference. As we age it appears that there are certain limits as to what we can achieve, but our net worth is not always in things. We have great wisdom that has been accumulated over a considerable number of years. Although that wisdom is not always sought out by the younger generation...all we need to do is make the deposit and allow them to take it as they wish. You can only lead a horse to water, but you can't make it take a drink. As people of wisdom - all we need to do is lead. All we need to do is make the deposit. Once upon a time the older males were the one who were being led. You may have been just as defiant as the young ones are today, but look at you now. You are your age even if you still appear to be young at heart. Age is not something to be ashamed of; it is something that is earned. Don't be afraid to accept your age.

No offense, but how many older men have you seen trying to act or look much younger than they are. The ironic thing is the fact that everyone knows they are acting, but them. They are trying to pull the wool over everyone's eyes, but the only one that is being fooled is the older guy trying to appear to be something that he is not. It is okay to be you. If you don't like your image, go ahead and work on it to a point, but if that means trying to pull off a great lie, no one is fooled, but the one who is fooling.

Swim as long as you can swim; dance as long as you feel like dancing. Run if you can, walk if you must; when your body feels tired let it rest. When you were young the body was full of youth, but as you age that youth burns out like the wick of a burning candle. No candle was made to last forever. It burns until it can't burn any more, then it is time for a new one. You are your age – there is nothing wrong with that. Carry it as a badge of honor. -Greg Middleton-

You are your age, even if it may appear otherwise. Such is life. When you were a child you acted and looked like a child, but as you aged you had to put away those childish things and become the adult you are.

STAND UP AND BE A MAN

We do a disservice to our boys today when we tell them that they are not to display their full range of human emotions. Sure there is a certain image that is perceived to be manlier than others, but that does not mean that men don't have, or that they should not express their emotions. It appears that the boys growing up in the NOW generation may not have as much problem as the ones earlier, because even during the baby boomer generation it was not common place for men to hug their sons or to tell them openly that they loved them. Instead, it was always, STAND UP AND BE A MAN.

In truth, men have deep emotions, and they have tear ducts; they are capable of expressing deep love and compassion for each other as well as their female partners. Today, best friends who are males hug each other in spite of what others may think. In some cultures men actually greet each other with a kiss on the cheeks. Why we make it taboo for men to show more emotions is beyond reasoning. A *real man* is not threatened by showing his emotions. It is only those on the outside who may have opinions or perceptions. Why live your life according to the shallow minds of others?

We are fortunate as men of today to see a lot of team sports on television. We see men excited about scoring and show such emotions by hugging each other and freely showing their happiness. We see guys slap each other on the behind as encouragement. What was once perceived as un-manly is now accepted as humanly. A *real man* of today should bring the total package. If he suppresses his emotions they will spill over into other things such as addictions or dysfunctional behaviors. Yes - we should STAND UP AND BE A MAN, but that means bringing the total package.

Fathers, learn to hug your boys. Husbands, learn to express your emotions with your spouses or partners. It is okay for a boy to play a violin or the flute or any musical instrument that he has the talents to perform. It is okay for boys to become dancers and to be graceful or limber. Even though there are perceived images that are manlier than others, let us not restrict our genuine talents and abilities because of what other people think. The dysfunction here is trying to deny who you are because you are trying to become what others want you to be. In the end, it will all come out in the wash. I'm not promoting anything here, but becoming the genuine person God made you to become without any undue pressure.

Chapter Eight

THE PROBLEM WITH MALES TODAY

Imagine a person who has a drinking problem. Until that person realizes they have a problem, very little would be done toward finding a cure. Imagine having an illness in your body. Very little would be done to seek healing until the person becomes aware they are ill. Even though the statistics show a notable decline in many areas of typical male functions, until we consciously admit that there is a problem very little will be done in order to fix anything. For this reason, this book along with many other ones like it, is being written and published. But, are we reaching our marketplaces? Are the people that need to read this material getting the message? The threshold of change has already happened, but it is time for people to become consciously aware of those changes and make the appropriate and necessary adjustments, and/or corrections.

Below are a few statistics of which we need to become aware. These statistics identify the problems males are experiencing today. They also forecast the new future if nothing changes.

LABOR STATISTICS

Table 16. **Median usual weekly earnings of full-time wage and salary workers in current dollars by race, Hispanic or Latino ethnicity, and sex, 1979-2007 annual averages**

Year	Total, both sexes					Women				
	Total	White	Black or African American	Asian	Hispanic or Latino ethnicity	Total	White	Black or African American	Asian	Hispanic or Latino ethnicity
1979......	$241	$248	$199	-	$194	$182	$184	$169	-	$157
1980......	262	269	212	-	209	201	203	185	-	172
1981......	284	291	235	-	223	219	221	206	-	190
1982......	302	310	245	-	240	239	242	217	-	203
1983......	313	320	261	-	250	252	254	232	-	215
1984......	326	336	269	-	259	265	268	241	-	223
1985......	344	356	277	-	270	277	281	252	-	230
1986 [1]....	359	371	291	-	277	291	294	264	-	241
1987......	374	384	301	-	285	303	307	276	-	251
1988......	385	395	314	-	290	315	318	288	-	260
1989......	399	409	319	-	298	328	334	301	-	269
1990 [1]....	412	424	329	-	304	346	353	308	-	278
1991......	426	442	348	-	312	366	373	323	-	292
1992......	440	458	357	-	321	380	387	335	-	302
1993......	459	475	369	-	331	393	401	348	-	313
1994 [1]....	467	484	371	-	324	399	408	346	-	305
1995......	479	494	383	-	329	406	415	355	-	305
1996......	490	506	387	-	339	418	428	362	-	316
1997 [1]....	503	519	400	-	351	431	444	375	-	318
1998 [1]....	523	545	426	-	370	456	468	400	-	337
1999 [1]....	549	573	445	-	385	473	483	409	-	348
2000 [1]....	576	590	474	$615	399	493	502	429	$547	366
2001......	596	610	491	639	417	512	522	454	563	388
2002......	608	623	498	658	424	529	547	473	566	397
2003 [1]....	620	636	514	693	440	552	567	491	598	410
2004......	638	657	525	708	456	573	584	505	613	419
2005......	651	672	520	753	471	585	596	499	665	429
2006......	671	690	554	784	486	600	609	519	699	440
2007......	695	716	569	830	503	614	626	533	731	473

See footnote at end of table.

Table 16. **Median usual weekly earnings of full-time wage and salary workers in current dollars by race, Hispanic or Latino ethnicity, and sex, 1979-2007 annual averages—Continued**

Year	Men					Women's earnings as a percent of men's				
	Total	White	Black or African American	Asian	Hispanic or Latino ethnicity	Total	White	Black or African American	Asian	Hispanic or Latino ethnicity
1979......	$292	$298	$227	-	$219	62.3	61.7	74.4	-	71.7
1980......	313	320	244	-	234	64.2	63.4	75.8	-	73.5
1981......	340	350	268	-	251	64.4	63.1	76.9	-	75.7
1982......	364	375	278	-	269	65.7	64.5	78.1	-	75.5
1983......	379	387	294	-	274	66.5	65.6	78.9	-	78.5
1984......	392	401	303	-	287	67.6	66.8	79.5	-	77.7
1985......	407	418	305	-	296	68.1	67.2	82.6	-	77.7
1986 [1].....	419	433	319	-	299	69.5	67.9	82.8	-	80.6
1987......	434	450	327	-	306	69.8	68.2	84.4	-	82.0
1988......	449	465	348	-	308	70.2	68.4	82.8	-	84.4
1989......	468	482	348	-	315	70.1	69.3	86.5	-	85.4
1990 [1].....	481	494	361	-	318	71.9	71.5	85.3	-	87.4
1991......	493	506	375	-	323	74.2	73.7	86.1	-	90.4
1992......	501	514	380	-	339	75.8	75.3	88.2	-	89.1
1993......	510	524	392	-	346	77.1	76.5	88.8	-	90.5
1994 [1].....	522	547	400	-	343	76.4	74.6	86.5	-	88.9
1995......	538	566	411	-	350	75.5	73.3	86.4	-	87.1
1996......	557	580	412	-	356	75.0	73.8	87.9	-	88.8
1997 [1].....	579	595	432	-	371	74.4	74.6	86.8	-	85.7
1998 [1].....	598	615	468	-	390	76.3	76.1	85.5	-	86.4
1999 [1].....	618	638	488	-	406	76.5	75.7	83.8	-	85.7
2000 [1].....	641	662	510	$685	417	76.9	75.8	84.1	79.9	87.8
2001......	670	689	529	732	440	76.4	75.8	85.8	76.9	88.2
2002......	679	702	524	756	451	77.9	77.9	90.3	74.9	88.0
2003 [1].....	695	715	555	772	464	79.4	79.3	88.5	77.5	88.4
2004......	713	732	569	802	480	80.4	79.8	88.8	76.4	87.3
2005......	722	743	559	825	489	81.0	80.2	89.3	80.6	87.7
2006......	743	761	591	882	505	80.8	80.0	87.8	79.3	87.1
2007......	766	788	600	936	520	80.2	79.4	88.8	78.1	91.0

[1] The comparability of historical labor force data has been affected at various times by methodological and conceptual changes in the Current Population Survey (CPS). For an explanation, see the Historical Comparability documentation provided at http://www.bls.gov/cps/eetech_methods.pdf.

NOTE: Beginning in 2003, estimates for the above race groups (white, black or African American, and Asian) include persons who selected this race group only; persons who selected more than one race group are not included. Prior to 2003, persons who reported more than one race were included in the group they identified as the main race. Data for 2000-02 are for the category Asians and Pacific Islanders. Starting in 2003, Asians constitute a separate category. For more information, see the Historical Comparability documentation. Data for Asians were not tabulated prior to 2000.

SOURCE: Current Population Survey, U.S. Department of Labor, U.S. Bureau of Labor Statistics.

*** *Please refer to the previous charts in order to verify the following summations made below.*

Just to see how things are changing comparatively for the genders, look at the median usual weekly earnings for full-time wage and salary workers. In **1979,** the average male earned $292 per week and the average female earned only 62.3% of his income, which would be approximately $182 per week. When you look at it by race, you will note that in 1979, white males earned more than the average, $298 per week, while Hispanic or Latino ethnicity earned an average of $219. Blacks earned $227. Interestingly, at that same time white women earned less than either black females who earned $217 per week, or Hispanic/Latino females who earned just over $209 per week. This was probably because there were less white women in the work force at that time.

Skip forward to the year **2007,** when the average male median usual weekly earnings for full-time workers jumped to $766 per week. White males earned more at $788 while Blacks earned $600, Asian $936 and Hispanic/Latino earned $520 per week on average. At the same time, women on average earned 80.2% of the average male income with White women earning $614.3, Blacks women earning $680.2 and Hispanic/Latino women earning just over $697.

Perhaps what this represents is the documented workers in the workforce, but the greatest change by the statistics (according to the tables) was the change in the Hispanic/Latino women workers. Their males were the lowest on the overall scale while the women were the top on the female scale. These were the statistics reported by: Current Population Survey, U.S. Department of Labor, United States Bureau of Labor Statistics. *I did not personally verify this study.*

What this shows is a decline in the disparity of wage earning with men compared to women, or perhaps more so, an incline in the wages paid to women. It shows that women are progressing at a higher rate than men. Much of this reflects the changes in the laws regarding employment practices over recent years and it shows us who is taking advantage of those changes. By these statistics, Black, Latino, and Hispanic women are taking the most advantage of the new laws and labor practices. Asian women had overtaken the advancements over white women for a while but just recently they have fallen slightly behind. Since we are currently in a global downturn of the economy, it is difficult to calculate the numbers simply because people of all races, genders, nationalities, and economic stature are losing jobs; a sign of the times, rather than the differences in people.

However, in roughly twenty-eight years there was a drastic change that occurred in the workplace. How would you imagine specific families were affected as a result of the increase of earnings with females? Naturally, with more income, women had more power, flexibility, and independence. They no longer had to totally depend upon a man to care for their needs. In the past, many women stayed in dysfunctional families mainly for economic reasons, but if they could find a way to support themselves and their children they no longer had to be attached to a dysfunctional male. Certainly the change in the labor practices greatly assisted females and their dependant families. The question becomes, what did that change do to males as a whole?

In a capitalistic society money (is) has power. It usually dominates the trends because people who have money and power usually are the ones who set the trends. Those who have very little money or power in a capitalistic society are usually on the lower end of the decision making process. If this shifting of the guards continues we will see a notable change among Black, Hispanic, and Asian families in America. With white America, although greatly impacted, there seems to be balancing of the resources and leveling of the advantage they once had without challenge. With a huge head start, this advantage in Whites will last many years before the scale of equality become balanced. That applies to the grand picture, but individuals are beginning to suffer because of laws that prohibit discrimination in hiring practices. The once, "King of the mountain," is no longer the unchallenged king.

If you visit the major universities across the country you will see more non-white male and female faces on campus than was the case during prior years. In fact, you will see a lovely rainbow of colors, cultures, ethnicities, and other distinctions. This shift will affect families and the way business will be handled over the near future. Will this be a positive change or will it affect us negatively? Only time will answer that question. Regardless of the effect, we should walk into such changes with our eyes open rather than closed. Perhaps it will be a great change that will improve our lives. As it is, women have always been the primary nurturers of our families for years. If they gain the power as well, perhaps we would become gentler and more compassionate people.

EDUCATIONAL STATISTICS

One of the ways to look at this picture is by viewing the national status dropout rate, specifically in the United States. These statistics are kept by the U.S. Department of Education Institute of Education Sciences. The report I cite was from information gathered through 2006. Based upon the economic trends up through 2009, the statistics could only have gotten worse because of the worldwide economic recession. The information cited here was from the period of 1972 through 2006, allowing you to see the trends more thoroughly. This information shows a trend in how males are functioning in our society. Though this material appears to be from a reliable source, I have not personally validated it, nor do I claim it to be factual. If anyone is interested in disputing this material they are free to do so. They are also free to gather their facts straight from the Census Bureau or another "reliable" source. With this disclaimer we can proceed.

Since **1972,** the event dropout rates declined from *6.1 to 3.8%*. If you look at these statistics by race, sex, or economic status you will see a very wide disparity. You will also notice fluctuations throughout the years due to various factors.

***Please refer to tables 3 and 4 of the charts below for your reference.

Table 3. Event dropout rates of 15- through 24-year-olds who dropped out of grades 10–12, by sex and race/ethnicity: October 1972 through October 2006

Year[2]	Total (percent)	Sex (percent)		Race/ethnicity (percent)[1]		
		Male	Female	White, non-Hispanic	Black, non-Hispanic	Hispanic
1972	6.1	5.9	6.3	5.3	9.5	11.2
1973	6.3	6.8	5.7	5.5	9.9	10.0
1974	6.7	7.4	6.0	5.8	11.6	9.9
1975	5.8	5.4	6.1	5.0	8.7	10.9
1976	5.9	6.6	5.2	5.6	7.4	7.3
1977	6.5	6.9	6.1	6.1	8.6	7.8
1978	6.7	7.5	5.9	5.8	10.2	12.3
1979	6.7	6.8	6.7	6.0	9.9	9.8
1980	6.1	6.7	5.5	5.2	8.2	11.7
1981	5.9	6.0	5.8	4.8	9.7	10.7
1982	5.5	5.8	5.1	4.7	7.8	9.2
1983	5.2	5.8	4.7	4.4	7.0	10.1
1984	5.1	5.4	4.8	4.4	5.7	11.1
1985	5.2	5.4	5.0	4.3	7.8	9.8
1986	4.7	4.7	4.7	3.7	5.4	11.9
1987	4.1	4.3	3.8	3.5	6.4	5.4
1988	4.8	5.1	4.4	4.2	5.9	10.4
1989	4.5	4.5	4.5	3.5	7.8	7.8
1990	4.0	4.0	3.9	3.3	5.0	7.9
1991	4.0	3.8	4.2	3.2	6.0	7.3
1992	4.4	3.9	4.9	3.7	5.0	8.2
1993	4.5	4.6	4.3	3.9	5.8	6.7
1994	5.3	5.2	5.4	4.2	6.6	10.0
1995	5.7	6.2	5.3	4.5	6.4	12.4
1996	5.0	5.0	5.1	4.1	6.7	9.0
1997	4.6	5.0	4.1	3.6	5.0	9.5
1998	4.8	4.6	4.9	3.9	5.2	9.4
1999	5.0	4.6	5.4	4.0	6.5	7.8
2000	4.8	5.5	4.1	4.1	6.1	7.4
2001	5.0	5.6	4.3	4.1	6.3	8.8
2002	3.6	3.7	3.4	2.6	4.9	5.8
2003	4.0	4.2	3.8	3.2	4.8	7.1
2004	4.7	5.1	4.3	3.7	5.7	8.9
2005	3.8	4.2	3.4	2.8	7.3	5.0
2006	3.8	4.1	3.4	2.9	3.8	7.0

[Interpret data with caution. Due to relatively large standard errors, estimates are unstable.

1 Beginning in 2003, respondents were able to identify themselves as being "more than one race." The 2003 through 2006 White, non-Hispanic and Black, non-Hispanic categories consist of individuals who considered themselves to be one race and who did not identify as Hispanic. The Hispanic category includes Hispanics of all races and racial combinations. Due to small sample sizes for some or all of the years shown in the table, American Indians/Alaska Natives and Asians/Pacific Islanders are included in the totals but not shown separately. The "more than one race" category is also included in the total in 2003 through 2006 but not shown separately due to small sample size.

2 Estimates beginning in 1987 reflect new editing procedures for cases with missing data on school enrollment items. Estimates beginning in 1992 reflect new wording of the educational attainment item. Estimates beginning in 1994 reflect changes due to newly instituted computer-assisted interviewing. For details about changes in the Current Population Survey (CPS) over time, please see Kaufman, Alt, and Chapman (2004). *Dropout Rates in the United States: 2001* (NCES 2005-046). U.S. Department of Education. National Center for Education Statistics. Washington, DC: U.S. Government Printing Office.

NOTE: The event dropout rate indicates the percentage of youth ages 15 through 24 who dropped out of grades 10–12 between one October and the next (e.g., October 2005 to October 2006). Dropping out is defined as leaving school without a high school diploma or equivalent credential, such as a General Educational Development (GED) certificate.

SOURCE: U.S. Department of Commerce, Census Bureau, Current Population Survey (CPS), October (1972–2006).

Table 4. Event dropout rates of 15- through 24-year-olds who dropped out of grades 10–12, by family income: October 1972 through October 2006

Year[2]	Total (percent)	Family income (percent)[1] Low	Middle income	High income
1972	6.1	14.1	6.7	2.5
1973	6.3	17.3	7.0	1.8
1974	6.7	—	—	—
1975	5.8	15.7	6.0	2.6
1976	5.9	15.4	6.8	2.1
1977	6.5	15.5	7.6	2.2
1978	6.7	17.4	7.3	3.0
1979	6.7	17.1	6.9	3.6
1980	6.1	15.8	6.4	2.5
1981	5.9	14.4	6.2	2.8
1982	5.5	15.2	5.6	1.8
1983	5.2	10.4	6.0	2.2
1984	5.1	13.9	5.1	1.8
1985	5.2	14.2	5.2	2.1
1986	4.7	10.9	5.1	1.6
d1987	4.1	10.3	4.7	1.0
1988	4.8	13.7	4.7	1.3
1989	4.5	10.0	5.0	1.1
1990	4.0	9.5	4.3	1.1
1991	4.0	10.6	4.0	1.0
1992	4.4	10.9	4.4	1.3
1993	4.5	12.3	4.3	1.3
1994	5.3	13.0	5.2	2.1
1995	5.7	13.3	5.7	2.0
1996	5.0	11.1	5.1	2.1
1997	4.6	12.3	4.1	1.8
1998	4.8	12.7	3.8	2.7
1999	5.0	11.0	5.0	2.1
2000	4.8	10.0	5.2	1.6
2001	5.0	10.7	5.4	1.7
2002	3.6	7.7	3.6	1.7
2003	4.0	7.5	4.6	1.4
2004	4.7	10.4	4.6	2.5
2005	3.8	8.9	3.8	1.5
2006	3.8	9.0	3.5	2.0

— Not available.

1 Low income is defined as the bottom 20 percent of all family incomes for the year; middle income is between 20 and 80 percent of all family incomes; and high income is the top 20 percent of all family incomes.

2 Estimates beginning in 1987 reflect new editing procedures for cases with missing data on school enrollment items. Estimates beginning in 1992 reflect new wording of the educational attainment item. Estimates beginning in 1994 reflect changes due to newly instituted computer-assisted interviewing. For details about changes in the Current Population Survey (CPS) over time, please see Kaufman, Alt, and Chapman (2004). *Dropout Rates in the United States: 2001* (NCES 2005-046). U.S. Department of Education. National Center for Education Statistics. Washington, DC: U.S. Government Printing Office.

NOTE: The event dropout rate indicates the percentage of youth ages 15 through 24 who dropped out of grades 10–12 between one October and the next (e.g., October 2005 to October 2006). Dropping out is defined as leaving school without a high school diploma or equivalent credential, such as a General Educational Development (GED) certificate.

SOURCE: U.S. Department of Commerce, Census Bureau, Current Population Survey (CPS), October (1972–2006).

Although the overall dropout rates have declined severely over the years, males still drop out of school more on average than females. Some studies show as much as 4 to 1 - males over females - in certain age groups or economic status, but this particular chart does not show that to be the case. If you go back to 1972, the male dropout rate was 5.9 males to 6.3 females. The very next year the rate was 6.8 males to 5.7 females. In all but eight of the thirty-four years, the male dropout rate was greater than the females: Those years were: 1972, 1975,1991, 1992, 1994, 1996, 1998 and 1999. In a few of the years, the margin was very slim and in two others they were even. This study only covers students between the ages of fifteen through twenty-four, who dropped out of the tenth through the twelfth grades. Perhaps the statistics regarding the younger males may tell a different story.

When you look at the dropout rate by race it is alarming. Looking at the numbers in ten year segments, you will note the overall dropout rate to be *6.1% in 1972*. Of those, Whites were 5.3%, Blacks 9.5% and Hispanics 11.2%. In *1982,* the overall rate was *5.5%*; Whites 4.7%, Blacks 7.8%, and Hispanics 9.2%. In *1992,* the overall was *4.4%*; Whites 3.7%, Blacks 5.0%, and Hispanics 8.2%. In *2002,* the overall was *3.6%*; Whites 2.6, Blacks 4.9%, and Hispanics 5.8%. Since 2002, it appears to be an increase across the board in all races after a gradual decrease. In *2006,* the overall rate was *3.8%*; Whites 2.9%, Blacks 3.8%, and Hispanics 7.0%.

If you just look at the different races over the years, the figures are even more staggering among the minority races. The following data is regarding the status dropout rates of ages sixteen through twenty-four, by sex and race/ethnicity from **October 1972 through October 2006,** in reference to the total population.

In **1972,** the ***national dropout rate*** was *14.6%*; Whites 12.3%, Blacks 21.3%, and Hispanics 34.3%. In *1982* the total was *13.9%*; Whites 11.4%, Blacks 18.3%, and Hispanics 31.7%. In *1992,* the total was *11.0%;* Whites 7.7%, Blacks 13.7%, and Hispanics 29.4%. In *2002,* the total was *10.5%*; Whites 6.5%, Blacks 11.3%, and Hispanics 25.7%. In *2006,* the total was *9.3*%; whites 5.8% Blacks 10.7%, and Hispanics 22.1%. During those thirty-four years, Hispanics had a high of 35.8 percent in 1988, Blacks a high of 22.9 percent in 1975 and Whites gradually decreased nearly all the years.

The dropout rates based upon *family income* show the *low income rate to be 14.1% in* **1972,** *middle income to be 6.7%,* and the *high income to be 2.5%.* In **1982,** it was *15.2% low incomes, 5.6% middle incomes,* and *1.8% high incomes.* In **1992,** it was *10.9% low incomes, 4.4% middle incomes, and 1.3% high incomes.* In **2002,** it was *7.7% low incomes, 3.6% middle incomes, and 1.7% high incomes.* On average the dropout rate for low income families is about four and one half times greater than their peers from high income families.

These reports show us that something is not equal about our educational system. Minorities are disproportionally suffering when it comes to being properly prepared for the job markets. Even though things are improving they are nowhere near equal. Something must be done to balance the scales or it will erupt in society, causing the entire body to suffer.

If you take these statistics regarding labor and education, higher income earners and the higher educated people are less likely to be caught by our penal systems. There is a direct correlation.

CRIME STATISTICS

In reference to the male problem we need to look at the entire body of males. If one segment of the body disproportionately suffers it changes the entire dynamic. If one male robs, steals, cheats, kills, or otherwise commits crimes against another... certainly their victims are not always within the same race, even though proximity does play a major factor in crimes committed. People tend to use the crime of convenience over very methodical planning. Most criminals rob the ones closest to them or commit other criminal activities within their own neighborhoods. It is not like Robin Hood, where a criminal would go out of their way to rob only from the rich. Most criminals are not that sophisticated until you get to the white collar criminals that are drawn toward crimes that the poor cannot manage. High level crimes take serious funds and ingenuity, two things that petty criminals lack.

A brief look at the US Department of Justice, Bureau of Justice Statistics, will reveal the most likely criminals, the victims, the assorted crimes, and facts regarding how the justice system works. The main issue here in reference to this material is: who the men are - and - how their actions affect humanity overall. If there are more men incarcerated in the penal system, that would mean that there are less men nurturing and otherwise caring for their families. Again, the numbers are staggering. We must see this as <u>our</u> problem rather than <u>their</u> problem, in reference to the poor, uneducated, or the less fortunate. When a member of the body suffers, the entire body suffers.

There are more recent figures available, but just take a look at some of the numbers as recorded in the year 2001. As of December 31, 2001 there were an estimated 5.6 million adults who had ever served time in State or Federal prison, including 4.3 million former prisoners and 1.3 million adults still in prison. Nearly one third of former prisoners were still under correctional supervision, including 731,000 on parole, 437,000 on probation and 166,000 in local jails. In 2001, 2.7% of the US population had served time in prison, up from 1.8% in 1991 and 1.3% in 1974.

The prevalence of imprisonment in 2001 was higher for black males (16.6%) and Hispanic males (7.7%) than for white males at 2.6%. Black female numbers were 1.7%, Hispanic females 0.7% and white females 0.3%.

Nearly two-thirds of the 3.8 million increase in the number of adults ever incarcerated between 1974 and 2001 occurred as a result of an increase in first incarceration rates; one third occurred as a result of an increase in the number of residents age eighteen and older.

They also looked into the lifetime likelihood of going to state or federal prison and projected these figures:

- If the rates remain the same, an estimated one out of every fifteen persons (6.6%) will serve time in a prison during their lifetimes.
- The chances of going to prison are higher for –men (11.3%) than for women (1.8%). By race; Blacks 18.6%, Hispanics 10% and for whites only 3.4%.

- Based upon current rates of first incarceration, an estimated 32% of black males will enter State of Federal prison during their lifetimes, compared to 17% of Hispanic males and 5.9% of white males.

Here is a summary a few of the stats accumulated through the year 2002. Although it does not tell the entire picture, it does show us what is happening in our society. I actually copied this directly from the **US Department of Justice, Bureau of Justice Statistics** website:

Characteristics of State Prison inmates

- Women were 6.6% of the State prison inmates in 2001, up from 6% in 1995.
- Sixty-four percent of prison inmates belonged to racial or ethnic minorities in 2001.
- An estimated 57% of inmates were under age 35 in 2001.
- About 4% of State prison inmates were not U.S. citizens at yearend 2001.
- About 6% of State prison inmates were held in private facilities at yearend 2001.
- Altogether, an estimated 57% of inmates had a high school diploma or its equivalent.
- Among the State prison inmates in 2000:
  — nearly half were sentenced for a violent crime (49%)
  — a fifth was sentenced for a property crime (20%)
  — about a fifth was sentenced for a drug crime (21%)

Characteristics of jail inmates Demographics

- Women were 12% of the local jail inmates in 2002, up from 10% in 1996.
- Jail inmates were older on average in 2002 than 1996: 38% were age 35 or older, up from 32% in 1996.
- More than 6 in 10 persons in local jails in 2002

were racial or ethnic minorities, unchanged from 1996.
- An estimated 40% were black; 19%, Hispanic, 1% American Indian; 1% Asian; and 3% of more than one race/ethnicity.

Conviction Offense

- Half of jail inmates in 2002 were held for a violent or drug offense, almost unchanged from 1996.
- Drug offenders, up 37%, represented the largest source of jail population growth between 1996 and 2002.
- More than two-thirds of the growth in inmates held in local jails for drug law violations was due to an increase in persons charged with drug trafficking.
- Thirty-seven percent of jail inmates were convicted on a new charge; 18% were convicted on prior charges following revocation of probation or parole; 16% were both convicted of a prior charge and awaiting trial on a new charge; and 28% were un-convicted.

Criminal History

- Fifty-three percent of jail inmates were on probation, parole or pretrial release at the time of arrest.
- Four in 10 jail inmates had a current or past sentence for a violent offense.
- Thirty-nine percent of jail inmates in 2002 had served 3 or more prior sentences to incarceration or probation, down from 44% in 1996.

Substance Use and Treatment

- Half (50%) of convicted jail inmates were under the influence of drugs or alcohol at the time of the offense, down from 59% in 1996.
- Three out of every four convicted jail inmates were alcohol or drugs-involved at the time of their current offense.
- Alcohol use at the time of the offense dropped from 41% (1996) to 35% (2002), while drug use dropped from 35% to 29%.
- Average sentence length of inmates serving their time in a local jail increased from 22 months in 1996 to 24 months in 2002.
- Time expected to be served in jail dropped from 10 months in 1996 to 9 months, in 2002

Family background

- Thirty-one percent of jail inmates had grown up with a parent or guardian who abused alcohol or drugs
- About 12 percent had lived in a foster home or institution.
- Forty-six percent had a family member who had been incarcerated.
- More than 50% of the women in jail said they had been physically or sexually abused in the past, compared to more than 10% of the men.

<u>Comparing Federal and State prison inmates</u>

- In 1997, Federal inmates were more likely than State inmates to be
  — women (7% vs. 6%)
  — Hispanic (27% vs. 17%)

— age 45 or older (24% vs. 13%)
— with some college education (18% vs. 11%)
— noncitizens (18% vs. 5%)

- In 2000, an estimated 57% of Federal inmates and 21% of State inmates were serving a sentence for a drug offense; about 10% of Federal inmates and 49% of State inmates were in prison for a violent offense.
- Violent offenders accounted for 53% of the growth in State prisons between1990 to 2000, drug offenders accounted for 59% of the growth in Federal prisons.

These statistics may tell us where the problems lie, but how can we fix a problem that is so deep? If money, time, and afford is not allocated, this problem will not fade away; it will only get worse. If this many Black men are incarcerated; this many are dying young because of certain illnesses that normally plague Black men; if they are financially on the lower end of the resources; and some are just unavailable for other reasons not covered in this study, what will this do to the Black family as a whole? What would the spillover from these statistics do to all races? The numbers for Hispanics are not that much better. How will this affect them, since they are the fastest growing segment of our population in America?

If we do not see ourselves as a nation of people we will not get healthy as a people. It matters not if you are White, Black, Hispanic, Asian, Hebrew, Jew, Indian, Persian, or other, if we do not treat our illness as a people we will not heal as a nation of people. Color and race should be one of the last lines we draw when it comes to fixing our nation. It was on the backs of color that this nation was built. This is just a fact of history. We simply need to fix what has been broken for so long, or face even deeper consequences as a nation of people.

Chapter Nine

THE RITE OF PASSAGE

Perhaps after seeing the aforementioned statistics regarding how we are evolving as people it is easier to understand the need to assist the coming generations as much as humanly possible. These numbers are not acceptable by any stretch of the imagination. As much as we are progressing technologically it appears that we are digressing socially. There is little reverence overall for people and life itself. We're becoming more selfish and self-absorbed in attitude, rather than becoming our brother's keeper. Instead of adhering to strict fundamental moral principles, we are leaning more toward; "To each his own," or, "I got mine so you have to get yours."

Selfishness is not, and never will be a positive trait when it comes to the socialization of a group. Even though we, especially in America, have many individual freedoms, having them does not give us the right to abuse each other. Freedom of choice cannot be equated equally with being a positive agent for the people. Choosing to abuse others goes against what we understand, as far as what it means to be a civilized nation. Even though people are free to do as they like, most selfish choices are not a positive force in the universe. However, since we know that the universe requires both positive and negative elements, the ability to choose either way is partly what makes us human beings. We are free-willed beings.

A person with no restrictions will gravitate toward what is natural within them. People don't just become nice, caring, and loving by nature. As members of the animal family we have basic instincts to take care of the self (self-preservation) over being morally sound. Good moral behaviors are learned and not necessarily inherited. Try placing infants in a closed environment, only giving them nourishment to sustain their life and nothing else; watch and see how they progress. They would revert to their basic animal instincts.

The sense of right and wrong is conditioned in us. Good behavior is conditioned in us. If you do not train a child in the ways you wish them to grow they will just become whatever is most natural to them. Basically, everything about how we have evolved as people is the result of some influence in our environment. *Good influences* assist us in learning good behaviors while *bad influences* assist us in developing bad behaviors. *No influences* at all will usually follow the laws of entropy. Just as an empty field usually grows wild weeds, untrained people become wild in nature. If you want a well manicured garden you will need to meticulously work on it. If you want children to adopt good and sound moral behavior you will need to meticulously work on them.

RITES OF PASSAGE DEFINED

The rites of passage typically consist of ceremonies that mark a person's progress from one role, (phase of life, or social status) to another. The term was first used by the Belgian anthropologist Arnold van Gennep. The basic life changes are birth, puberty, marriage, and death. Each change is marked by a transitional period involving specific rituals: removal of the individual from his or her former status; suspension from normal social contact; and readmission into society in the newly acquired status. This transitional process sometimes provides others with the opportunity to adjust to the event, as for example, the death of a loved one. Rites of passage occur in all societies and often involve symbolism, and reaffirm the values of a society.

The various stages listed in this particular article consisted of birth, puberty, marriage, menopause, and death. This information was taken from an article written by Donald F. Tuzin, M.A., Ph.D., Professor of Anthropology, University of California in San Diego. The full article can be found through the Internet at this link: http://encarta.msn.com/encyclopedia_761557678_2/Rites_of_Passage. html.

In the west, this tradition is not practiced as much by most Americans, but there are a few races or ethnicities that maintain their tradition and follow such practices. For example, puberty rites generally require initiates to be instructed in the etiquette, arts, and folklore of their society, in preparation for the conditions of full adulthood. The Jewish ceremony of <u>bar mitzvah</u> for a boy, or <u>bat mitzvah</u> for a girl, marks the passage of a young person into adulthood after a period of prescribed religious instruction. Many other races practice some sort of ceremony welcoming a child into their adult stage.

As boys and girls reach the stage of puberty, they literally turn from a child to a reproducing human adult. However, just the ability to reproduce does not usually make one an "adult." Obviously, different cultures use different age markers in order to determine what is considered to be a legal adult. Even still, just legal age or the ability to reproduce is not all it takes to become a matured adult capable of making sound and solid rational decisions based upon prudence.

In reference to the legal or technical definition of what makes one an adult, you would need to know the various laws or customs of the people who make such determinations. However, when it comes to the making of what we are calling a *real man*, we need to define, or redefine what we consider that to mean. Is a *real man* one that reaches a particular age? Is a *real man* one who has the ability to father a child? Regarding this specific subject matter, becoming a *real man*, neither age nor the ability to produce and inject sperm makes a *real man*. A *real man* must also come with character. If you live long enough you can become what is called a man. If you engage in sex as a healthy male you can more than likely produce offspring, but is that worthy of being called a "real" man? This is the subject this book is trying to address. Being a *real man* requires more than producing sperm and age.

BECOMING CHAMELEONS

A chameleon is reptile that has the ability to mimic his immediate surroundings. This allows him protection against his predators. While in green leaves they turn green. While on brown bark they turn brown. In their natural environments they can mimic most things they cross over in their environment, perhaps with the exception of water or something invisible.

Many animals will stay with their parents, even if it is for just a short while, in order that they may learn enough to take care of themselves. For some animals it is a very short period. For others it is much longer. Human beings probably have the longest period before the parent actually "kicks them out of the nest." During the period while a child, or animal, is with the parent, they learn by watching them act or do things and repeat what they see. By mimicking the adults, most animals learn how to behave and become independent, capable of caring for themselves.

Fortunately for most animals, this is not a sophisticated thought process. They do what they do naturally by instinct and their offspring learn from what is natural within their species. With only a few exceptions this process is more instinctual than it is philosophical or intellectual. Even though dolphins and some primates seem to use logical processes that appear to mimic the ability to reason, most of it is a learned response and not an act of volition. Even elephants can remember where their watering holes are - they do not know how to package water and save it for a rainy day. They don't seem to know how to hide the water so other animals cannot find their precious water source. In essence, the ability to make rational or irrational decisions, or the ability to make either good or bad choices, seems to be unique to human beings. Because of this God-given ability we must teach our young in the ways that they should grow so as they mature, that is what they become.

There are several similarities between human beings and other animals. Most welcome their young and are quite protective of them. Since we have the ability to bring children into the world by choice, some of the circumstances we choose to bring children into the world were not calculated or intended. Some children come into the world strictly by accident. Not all children are wanted or welcomed simply because we have the ability to choose how we feel about having children. Unplanned pregnancies can be a very negative experience for both the mother and the father. Such attitudes can greatly influence the amount of love these parents may give to that child. Even though you would think the rite of birth would not be a subjective act, we have the ability to make it so.

If children are unwanted and not loved they can sense that with their inner sensory abilities. A child growing up in an environment where there is no love will usually mimic what he or she sees or senses. If there is resentment coming from the parent to the child, that energy may become a part of that child's overall personality trait. Although such traits may not be visibly seen in the child, they become a part of his or her inner being.

People considering bringing children into the world, or even committing the act that could bring children into the world, should think reverently before they make such decisions. A child should have the right (rite) to be born into a world that wants them. Shame on those who do not accept this "rite" seriously!

FATHERLY RESPONSIBILITY

Even though the rite of passage is not specific to males alone, this book is talking about becoming a *real man* and discussing the qualities that should entail. A *real man* is one that accepts complete responsibility for his children as well as all other responsibilities that are entrusted to him. He appropriately trains himself so he is qualified to be hired in the job market. He properly cares for his spouse, aging parents, and those who need him as well. In essence, he is the head over all that life places in front of him. He (a real man) bears that responsibility with pride and privilege.

Being a father has a wide range of responsibilities of which parenting is only one of many. We have always heard that the father is also the protector and a major provider for the family. Although the role of primary provider may be altering because of women in the workplace, this does not excuse males from what they must do as well. When it comes time for a boy to become a man it is the father's responsibility to teach him as best he can in order to assure that boy progresses properly into manhood. This is not a law or even an accepted custom in our country by the majority of people, but still, it is a God-given responsibility. Unfortunately too many men shirk their responsibilities.

Perhaps at one point in time men considered fatherhood much more reverently than they do today. The earlier generations seemed to have planted that moral sense of responsibility in the subsequent generation as a rite of passage. It was not always necessary to have a formal ceremony in order to pass on this torch. It was just part of your responsibility as a parent to pass this on to your children. This feeling of responsibility was something that was conditioned in most people. If people aren't taught responsibility they usually don't know or accept it. Once people are taught things, at least they become aware of its existence. How is a boy or girl to learn things if he or she is not taught? It does not fall into them by osmosis.

To be quite clear about this, not all men are *real men*, nor do all men make good fathers. Not all men respond to the same stimulus or teaching. Many men had no role models that took the time to teach them manly behaviors. Fatherly responsibility doesn't appear to be a natural trait among male humans as it appears to be with many other animals. Some animals seem to protect their own, even to death. Some male animals will even kill other offspring that are not of his own blood in order to capture the females and make them submissive to their male dominant control, such as the lion. They do this in order to insure their bloodlines. With human males it appears to be quite subjective and depends solely upon individual conditioning and training. If a male has no training, apparently he has no natural fatherhood instincts. However, if he has good character he more than likely will figure out how to become a good father even if it wasn't taught to him directly. Again, the measure of a man is not in things, but more in character, because with it he can make the necessary adjustments to the cards that are dealt to him.

CHANGE IN THE DYNAMIC OF FATHERS

As we take a look at boys who grew up after the social revolution of the 1960s and 70s, you will note a substantial difference in them compared to the ones called the baby boomers. The baby boomer generation was taught from the "old school" method, which essentially meant that you had to be prepared to work hard for a living in order to support yourself and your families. They were also taught to value education and training along with learning how to develop sound life principles. Since the previous generation before the boomer generation had faced and survived the great depression of the 1930s, they learned basic values, such as how to sustain one's self through tough times. This is what they instilled in the baby boomer generation. This training does not appear to be as prevalent in the subsequent generations.

If you look back through our history, approximately every twenty years there is a new generation coming into life. If you start from the early 1900's, men were just learning how to adjust to technological advances. The automobile was invented in 1903. Prior to that transportation was horse power or steam engines, or just man power. In the 1920s, the automobiles were flourishing and life was on an uprising called the roaring twenties. This ended with the great depression of the 1930s. The next generations were those born in the 1940's. They came onboard just after the great depression and ended through World War II. That was a turbulent time for people who were born through that phase of time. The next generation was born in the 1960's, the age of tremendous social revolution; the hippies and the flower children. Next, you had the children of the 1980's, who faced technology as never seen before so rapidly.

This brings us to those born in the new millennium, the 2000's. So far, this generation has yet to show its unique characteristics. They have the privilege of clearly seeing the past one hundred years of mankind in action. What a daunting task to see that much change in such a brief period of time, compared with the rest of our long recorded history. We have gone from horse driven wagons to space shuttles working in outer space. No other generations had that much change to adjust to in such a brief period. It is almost as though a person could be born and die and still not adjust to the life that came at them.

If boys are to become and succeed as fathers they will need our assistance. We need to teach them from the very rich tradition from which we have seen or known about. If the males born today are to become *real men,* it will be because we gave them a solid foundation. Never before in the history of recorded time has this much wisdom been imparted upon our planet in such a relatively short period of time. We are the torch bearers. Like a relay race, it is our job to pass on the torch. If we drop the torch our boys cannot become the sort of men that we learned to become from fathers and forefathers. The rite of passage is not just a rite but more of a responsibility as well.

Chapter Ten

THE FUTURE OF MAN-kind

No one has a crystal ball that can accurately predict the future. Nonetheless, there are enough indicators to show us the direction in which things are headed so we can make the proper adjustments and precautions. In today's world of meteorology we can predict where weather patterns are forming and where they may be headed fairly well. With this foreknowledge people who are in the path of a potential storm can take the proper precautions and possibly avoid certain dangers. That is what it is like with the indicators we see today in society, specifically with males and the male/female dynamic. The storm clouds are already forming and headed in a particular direction. We can forecast with great certainty that if nothing is done to alter the current direction, a major change in the roles and relationships between men and women will definitely change significantly in the near future.

In truth, the future of mankind is in the hands of men. How the next few generations deal with this male issue has a lot to do with how males handle their responsibilities. If they pass it on properly, men of the future will be healthy. Presently, the new flock appears to be like a deer caught in the headlights. We have the power and ability to educate them and make them fully aware. We need to teach them well in the "here and now" so once the torch is passed on properly, they will be fully equipped to handle whatever challenges may arise in the future. After we have done our parts we must trust them to do theirs' just as we did ours.

Many of us will not be around to see the next show. That will be exclusively for them and their offspring. It is like fixing up a classic car and turning the keys over to your son, after you had put so much time and afford into perfecting your crown jewel. Once he has the keys it is no longer your classic, or your potential problem.

RISE IN CONSCIOUSNESS

We live in an age where it is more difficult to be uninformed than it is to be informed. In the olden days the majority of people did not know how to read, write, or otherwise assimilate knowledge. It was not as easy for them to grasp knowledge in order to become consciously aware of their surroundings. Since the majority of people were not well-educated, the level of consciousness was kept at a low threshold. That is no longer the case. Things have changed tremendously in these modern times. Even if a person didn't know how to read they could simply turn on the radio, television, cell phones, email, text screens, or just look up at pictures on billboards and become aware. We no longer have to dig in order to find knowledge because the advertisers find ways to bring it to us where we live, work, and play.

Our planet is becoming increasingly much smaller. We hear of things happening around the world on the evening news shortly after they actually happened. Just over a century ago the pony express had to deliver the news that may have taken months or years. Now we get it within seconds or minutes. If there is a revolt in Iran we know about it from people who text it out or use social networking like Facebook, Twitter, Myspace, or the like. Nothing is hidden! We can actually look down from the satellites parked in outer space and/or Google just where the event is happening, as it is happening. This is an entirely new age we are living. People, including men, have to make themselves informed or life will pass them by before they knew they were actually living.

We can say with great certainty that people are becoming more aware because that is the age we live within; the age of awareness. We should also be able to say that people are becoming more consciously aware, but that is not necessarily the case. Consciousness is deeper than just being aware of the existence of something. Consciousness denotes a deeper awareness and understanding, not only of the things around you, but also of the purposes they serve. It is more like being alert and paying attention to what is happening rather than just knowing something is happening around you. If you are married and with children you are aware that you have children and they are around you, but are you consciously aware of what is happening in their lives? Do you spend quality time with your children in order to know what is happening in their lives? Just knowing that something exists and being consciously aware are two different things.

The only way people become consciously aware is by making it a priority. If they seek knowledge, more than likely, they will find it. In the same way, if they do not seek knowledge it usually does not come into them by osmosis, even though it is still harder to be uninformed than it is to be informed because of technology. This takes us back to basic life principles that have endured through time and technological changes.

Spiritual and/or religious practices have existed for nearly as long as we have been on the planet. It has certainly been around for as long as we have been keeping recorded history. Printed material such as the Holy Bible and other sacred Holy Scriptures, from several world renowned religions, are available to anyone who has an interest in acquiring spiritual knowledge. We have this precious information because great enlightened men from times past recorded it in writing in order to pass the torch on to the subsequent generations. They passed on certain practices that would assist us more with our humanity and spirituality rather than just our material status. They were more concerned about you as a spirit-being rather than your physical wellbeing. These practices have transcended time and are still a valid resource capable of improving lives. With this deep inner knowing comes awareness and the ability to actually practice a set of skills that will make a positive impact upon how life manifests. Because so few people seem to be interested in surfing as deep into the spiritual aspect of their being, they end up living more on the surface of life and never really incorporate its true deeper meaning.

This brings the question of how consciousness is assimilated within society. Are the *few* responsible for the *masses*? Can spiritual awareness be forced upon the people? The answer to the first question is yes, the few does end up becoming in some way responsible for the masses. This has been the primary method of learning throughout our human evolution. Brave individual pioneers reach out and explore new areas in order to open the doors to others who eventually follow through. Likewise, individual inventors come up with new innovations and create new products and services that are shared with the entire human race. It has always been the few that have opened doors for the masses. Perhaps part of this is by divine design, but in each generation there are a few gifted and chosen people who seem to have the necessary seed to grow us as a species.

Through waves of consciousness that float in the universe, knowledge is always available and circling. However, it requires the ability of the gifted ones to pick up (receive) these waves of consciousness and bring them into manifestation. Inventors intuitively sense things and bring them into being. Gifted artist and creative minds sense things intuitively and bring them into being. As a species we are ever evolving primarily because of the gifted few. This is the nature of human kind.

Regarding spiritual awareness being forced upon the people, very seldom can you force people to accept what they are unwilling to accept. You may force certain behaviors or means of control over them strictly from a power base, but that doesn't mean that people inwardly accept such domination against their will. In order to get people to accept change it is best to present them with an option of which they are willing to accept and allow them to change their own mind because of understanding a better alternative. With this stated, we know about religious and other persecution that has always existed in mankind. The will of the people has always been vulnerable to the will of the more powerful, aggressive, or more assertive. In order for people to grow inwardly, they must take a firm stand regarding their entire being; physically, mentally, emotionally, and spiritually. In order to raise the consciousness level, individuals must first understand their total being and learn how it works.

YOU ARE THE RECEIVER

If you see yourself as the receiver of frequencies you will better understand the nature of consciousness. It is like tuning your radio to a particular frequency in order to listen to your favorite station. You

97

are the same sort receiver with capabilities of receiving divine knowledge from the universe. As information is being transmitted universally you have the ability to capture this knowledge. The key is learning how to properly tune your channel selector in order to screen out the garbage (spam) and capture the goods. Not all information in the airwaves is good or beneficial.

Since much of our population does not appear to be aware of the divine knowledge that is constantly being transmitted, we are not progressing as well as possible. Remember, consciousness awareness is a deeper, inner-knowing than just being aware of the existence of things. Until more people desire to surf deeper, we will remain more at the basic level of life rather than exploring its more refined possibilities. Obviously there is so much more available that we have not even begun to explore. Probably the least explored part of our humanity is the inner spiritual workings, rather than the outer physical things that the eye can see. It is like looking at the exposed portion of an iceberg. The larger part is under the water line. In order to explore this deeper vein people will have to desire it.

If you are not aware that you have parts that serve a specific purpose, chances are you will not go out of your way to build upon an aspect of which you have no awareness. Your intuitiveness and other traits come through your spiritual aspect. If you do not recognize having a spiritual aspect it will not serve you to its optimum capacity. Many times just becoming knowledgeable of things may bring awareness to the forefront. Nonetheless, becoming consciously aware gives you the ability to apply knowledge to practical living. Through religion and other spiritual practices people are able to refine their spiritual powers. They actually increase their capacity to receive things or signals that were always transmitting. However, if one were not properly aligned to receive such frequencies, the signals would have floated over with little consequence. Once you are tuned or otherwise aligned with such universal frequencies they are drawn to you, simply because you become the receiver (magnet) that attracts them.

A *real man* knows of such things and will seek to become the best he can be. To be ignorant in the face of knowledge is not an indication of a *real man*. To be belligerent for no clear reason or to intentionally block the knowledge given by the universe (God) is not a person aligned with truth. Truth is a stable force that exists within the universe. If one does not align themselves with truth, they exist outside of what is natural. If males do not align themselves with their natural purpose, and instead they go against the natural flow; they become more a part of the problem rather than an aid in the solution. Currently, males need to realign themselves with nature's purpose, design, and intent. This is what appears to be lost. Males have fallen out of their natural alignment. It is like an automobile that is out of tune. Once the car is tuned up properly it will run more efficiently. The male gender seems to be out of tune.

ACCEPT TOTAL RESPONSIBILITY

Many people find themselves in an adverse situation and quickly blame exterior forces for their predicament. Yes, there are many reasons why people fail or fall short of the mark, but if you allow those reasons to have the power over you they will continue to control you. On the other hand, once you take full responsibility the power to change is in your control: "The buck stops here!" If someone makes you mad and you hold them responsible for being mad, then you have given them the power over you. Instead, if someone makes you mad and you choose to ignore them, forgive them, or forget them - the power is within your control. The same is true about any condition or circumstance of which you hold others responsible. Determine who has the power. You should!

If you blame being Black, Hispanic, or another minority race as a reason why you aren't successful then "they," powers that be, have the power over you. If you accept your race, culture, or economic statue as your birthright and/or responsibility, then no one has power over you. If you wish to break through previous boundaries, then you will no longer see people as your adversaries; they merely become obstacles to be overcome. If a tree falls across the road you are traveling it is senseless to blame the tree. You are free to blame the tree, but what "good" would it do? It is merely an obstacle that must be overcome. Allowing people, circumstances, or things to have power over you gives them your power. Accepting full responsibility for your being places the power back in your hands. A *real man* properly tuned to universal truth assumes full responsibility for himself and those of whom are entrusted to his manhood.

DIVINE DESIGN

There will come a day when a man does not need to be apologetic or ruthless about being male. Being male is a birthright that comes with certain responsibilities and/or divine purposes. God, or whatever you deem to be the source of creation, dealt the cards – we must play the hand that we were dealt. If you are male that choice was made at birth, however, the fact that you are male is by design and intentional. Likewise, females are born with certain traits, talents, gifts, and abilities that are not the same as males. They should fully accept their natural selection as well and accept the responsibilities that come with being born female.

The issue (clash) between the genders seems to be more in ego-based perceptions, rather than biology, in most cases. Each gender does not appear to be getting the respect warranted so they fight back against the other gender. When both find themselves competing for resources and/or position it becomes a competitive battle, rather than people trying to do what they do best for the sake of improvements. If both genders would concentrate upon what they do well and fully respect the opposite gender for their specialties, there shouldn't be a conflict. However, when egos become threatened people do things to protect their egos rather than the primary items of importance. In order to do what is better for the people, the family, and for society over all, genders should work cohesively with each other rather than treating each other as adversaries. Strangely, this adversarial behavior seems to be most prominent in marriage, where parties actually take sacred vows to love and honor each other. Why is it so hard for couples, who vow to assist one another to be at least civil with each other?

A PEEK AHEAD IN THE FUTURE

In the future gender clashes should tone down. Just as water always seems to find the path of the least resistance, the roles of the genders will take care of themselves. Currently, both genders seem to be jockeying for position, but nature will prevail in the end. Even though a few individuals will always seek to fulfill their personal agendas, males will always need, and pursue females. Females in turn will always desire, and need males, but they will not depend upon them in the same way as in the past. Women will be more than capable of getting pregnant and delivering a child without direct intercourse from a male. We already have the technology to use artificial insemination, even using frozen sperm in order to impregnate females. Females can go to a sperm bank and select certain features they want in a child and fulfill that order. Sperm banks are becoming more efficient in keeping a databank on certain features from the male's genes and DNA.

With technology, people will have control more over the birth selections and process. Unfortunately, the rich and wealthy will always have more controls and abilities than the poor. As we look further into the work that is being done with stem cells, we will have the ability to manipulate the birth of children even more toward the desires of the paying clients. Perhaps this will produce healthier babies that are more desirable and loved. On the other hand, if people continue to reveal the flaws of human nature we may be looking at *meat markets* or *making babies for hire*. Something about that does not sound natural! With these new technological advances comes an even deeper responsibility to establish and hold on to high moral codes and values.

Although men will be needed to create the sperm necessary for birth, there will never be a shortage of men willing to donate them for a price. People will do nearly anything for profit. Unfortunately, the desire to have babies has created a business of men producing sperm for hire and even women leasing out their wombs to carry embryos for the entire birth term. Although such services may be needed in some cases when there is infertility with one or both partners, the ability to produce babies for hire follows the desires of those who are willing and able to pay for certain services. If a woman does not want to go through the nine-month pregnancy process she can simply hire a surrogate mother to do that for her. Such services will be used more and more by gay couples who wish to produce and raise children. At this point, we still do not know how all this change will affect the way we operate as a race.

As we project ahead, it appears that males will become the minority or the subservient gender for at least a period of history, because of the female's ability to do many things independently. Unlike in the past, females are preparing themselves better for the coming job markets than males. They will no longer necessarily have to have a man in order to have and raise a family. If they become the major bread earner they will be able use their financial advantage in order to control certain ineffective or non-producing males. Just as men were once considered disposable because of the nature of war, this time they will be disposable if they are not capable of standing up to the credentials of the superior females.

More women will be in positions of power, which will reverse the hiring practices of the past. Just as men were more pro-male in hiring practices of the past, perhaps women will lean toward hiring more women. It will not be because of gender discrimination, but because they will be the better candidate for the jobs. However, this will be a short lived superiority for females, because as the supply of men is lessoned, the demand will be higher. Men will regain their power simply because of supply and demand: The lesser the supply – the greater the demand.

Unfortunately, there will always be a tug of war between the sexes, but the reasons for the battle will change over time. The days when both sexes lay down their arms and make love over war will be few but cherished by both sides. No one loves the war games; however, until the consciousness of mankind improves...egos will instigate gender battles.

For the immediate and subsequent generations males will notice a severe downturn, but because men are warriors by nature that downturn will be brief. Men will get their acts back together and understand the value of proper education and training in order to compete for the tasks at hand. Since males are competitors by nature, they will rise to the occasion once they realize they are in competition.

This *lazy male syndrome* will be short lived because males were not created to be soft and weak creatures. The need to burn energy vigorously will drive men back into action. With the loss of hard manual labor jobs in the workforce, men will need to create alternative ways of burning energy in order to control their flow of testosterone.

In order to compete for the most desirable females, men will not only have to be smart, but also physically fit as well. This natural competition is what will fuel men ahead once again more toward gender equality. Once the scales are balanced between the sexes it will only fluctuate slightly as each gender jockey for position over time.

***THIS IS MERELY A FORECAST OF WHAT MAY HAPPEN IN THE NEAR FUTURE IF CHANGES ARE NOT MADE TO ALTER THE EXISTING TRENDS THAT ARE IN PROGRESS.

Chapter Eleven

WHAT MEN NEED NOW

This chapter is different from chapter eight where we basically identified much of the problem earlier. Now we need to come up with more solutions to the problems, rather than mere recognition; even though recognition is an important part of the healing process. In order to make a substantial dent in the problem, men need to take an individual and assertive stand to fix what they see broken right in front of them. They need to work on their marriages if they are not functioning properly. They need to become better fathers if they know that are not giving their all to the children. They need to address any problem that they know about and make themselves better overall as a person. What men need now it to adopt the theory of "each one - teach one." If every man takes the responsibility for himself that alone would be a great gain.

Although universal consciousness is something that is very real... men don't need to spend their immediate time doing things that produce less than what is spent. We need to work on value added things that produce immediate returns. If you do not know how to communicate well with your spouse it may require the services of professionals, but in the meanwhile you can start by being more sympathetic and aware of the power you are enforcing over your mates. Men say really harsh and even mean things without even realizing they may be doing so. The way the average man thinks is not conducive to what the average woman feels. Women operate more from their feelings while guys operate more from what they think. If this adjustment is not taken into consideration, men and women will remain on separate pages and not know why.

In the long run, men need to understand women better, and definitely women need to understand men better, but in the meanwhile, much can be gained by using common sense rather than operating by the seat of our pants. When we blurt out things before the mind is engaged we may say harsh things, but becoming impeccable with our tongues as a way of operation will assist us in thinking more carefully before we speak. Most women will sense when you are being more thoughtful and reward you in some way or another, or NOT! Even if there is no reward - becoming a better person is a reward in and of itself. Learning to be more sensitive or compassionate to and with females is not a bad trait to learn. Again, if you are looking at winning and losing you are focusing on the wrong picture. Instead, seek peace and pursue it with all you have to offer.

Even though this chapter may be a reiteration of things we have already mentioned before, there are certain things and behaviors that need highlighting. The goal of a *real man* is to become a better functional person that just happens to be male. It has nothing to do with competing with females or even competing with other males. When we seek to become better human beings everybody wins. We need to find ways to work on ourselves while honoring the fact that we are males by birth. If society is confused about the issue or the exact role a *real man* should exemplify…we don't have to be confused just because the majority is confused. We have a general idea of what a real man should exemplify. However, if we are waiting on public approval before we act, all the cows will be out of the pasture while the gate is standing open. We already have inner powers that will assist us in changing and becoming better persons; one power being just plain common sense.

Even though this book wasn't written endorsing a specific religion, it is important that men find a practice that can assist them in improving the quality of their lives. Having a religion that doesn't make you a better person seems fruitless. If you are going through rituals and traditions, yet still having major problems in dealing with people and/or life in general… I would question the validity or reality of that practice. This is not intended as a knock against any particular religion. Remember… your religion is not what necessarily changes you; it is your desire to become a better person that yields to a better way or even a higher spirit that transforms you once you have committed to becoming better. This altering spirit already lives in you, but it requires your activation in order to serve you in ways that are not merely physical, but spiritual as well.

What men need now is a <u>new attitude</u> and a <u>new mindset</u> that is based upon current reality and not upon myth and old wives' tales. Much of what we learned as men was passed down by sources that were not necessarily reliable or authoritative. For example, many things we learned about the opposite sex were from boys our own age that had just as little or less experience than we had. It was a case of the blind leading the blind and egos puffing up to prove you were better than your partners. This was not education. Unfortunately, many men are still just an older version of those young, uneducated boys that have never gone back to set the record straight. There are encyclopedias of information already written on what we don't know or understand about women. If you want the facts, get them from a better authoritative source.

Since <u>not</u> all men enjoy reading, most do enjoy spending quality time with other males doing fun things for enjoyment's sake. Men need to learn to share their experiences with each other in order to assist each other when they have problems that require assistance. The problem is that men are taught to hold things on the inside rather than speaking about them openly. This old system does not work. Our foolish male pride causes us more harm than it does us good. We will need to learn to swallow our pride and reach out for assistance when needed.

When it comes to establishing ground rules in relationships, most of the boundary lines are set in the beginning stages of a relationship, whether intentionally or unintentionally. If you do not lay down firm lines in the beginning, don't expect to draw them later after the relationship is formed. You are free to expect them, but respecting them is a different matter.

During the courting stage both sexes usually reveal only their best sides. The fear of losing a good catch usually causes both parties to avoid showing the (real deal) truth. However, in real life situations your true sides will be exposed. When you are challenged and forced to react in ways that are not consistent with what you previously established...you should not be surprised if, or when it (the truth)) is met with strong resistance.

By the same token, women are just as guilty, if not more, of not laying their boundaries in the beginning of relationships as well. Because women are more concerned about vanity – men usually do not see the *real deal* until much later into the relationship - long after the boundary lines were drawn. Women are just as interested in getting a mate to make a commitment first. Because of this they are willing to forego the technicalities of establishing personal boundary lines. When the man crosses such a line, either accidentally or on purpose, it usually always gets sharp resistance. Since this line had never been discussed it normally leads to an argument.

To men this feels like a punch below the belt, but to women they think men should know such unknown and never-discussed issues. Because couples don't learn how to disagree with each other during such conflicting times, these invisible lines have been known to totally destroy marriages or relationships. Men need to understand this about establishing boundary lines and make adjustments to realities - if that is possible. At times these gender differences may be too severe to overcome. This is why they are called irreconcilable differences. If people cannot work out their issues, then it may be best to respectfully agree to part ways. Unfortunately, the parting of the ways seems to become vicious and uncharacteristic of people of character. Even in divorce people should remember that they are still people who just do not get along or agree. To treat another person with cruelty or evil is not a good human trait: divorce or not.

THE AGING PROCESS OF WINE

I am told that a great bottle of wine has to be properly seasoned. As it ages the true character comes out. Connoisseurs that have such exquisite taste buds can appreciate matured wines. I, on the other hand can drink the garden variety and achieve my purpose for far less money.

Relationships usually require a similar aging process. People need to grow together and learn to understand each other's strengths and weaknesses. The chances of meeting the perfect person that matches your character in every way is very slim. Even though the parties may be great individuals apart, they may have certain likes and dislikes that clash with each other. For example, if one party likes it hot and the other likes it cold that would be hard to accept unless both parties were willing to accept warm. If a person is willing to compromise it makes relationships easier to manage. If one party always insists upon having their way it makes it harder on the other party that always has to bend over backward. Being conscious of the other person's needs is part of what it means to be in a relationship. If the relationship is always tilted toward one side, eventually problems will brew. This depends upon the tolerance level of the person who is doing the most bending.

Too many relationships end before they even start the aging process. Obviously some people are more self-absorbed or selfish, so they are unwilling to give an inch. If you are in a relationship with such a person, you should question whether this is the right one for you. Unless you like being submissive or subservient, it will eventually take a toll on the soul. When the inner person is unhappy it puts a damper on the whole person. Real love has no desire to see the other person suffer. If you are doing things that you know irritate your mate − just don't do it. If such things are preformed outside your boundary lines then question the reason you are in that particular relationship.

In today's culture most problem marriages would destroy themselves in the first five years. By that time couples would know if they are well-suited for each other, or not. Unfortunately, such brief encounters did not last long enough for the seasoning process to work between the two parties. In previous days people may have even stayed together longer than it was profitable. It was not that marriages were that much better, but that people took their commitments more seriously.

There were people that waited even twenty years before they decide to call it quits. In such cases their tolerance level may have been high, or they waited until the kids were grown before calling it quits. They may have been too embarrassed of what others would think if they actually got a much-needed divorce. Even with seasoning and the aging process some marriages can't withstand the test of time. Many times this is because people don't understand the nature of relationships. In spite of the passage of time, there are some people who seem to defy nature and remain ignorant with the passage of time. Some even become more defiant or stubborn with time. When people stop working on themselves they may grow apart. If one party constantly works on self-improvements and the other remains the same, it may cause a rift to appear.

If one party decides to quit drinking or smoking after many years and the other doesn't then they may drift apart. People need to understand, not only their partner, but the nature of relationships as well. If they do nothing to keep the relationship refreshed it may grow stale and boring. Good relationships require constant tuning and refreshing. If you get to be each other's habit that does not make a great relationship. Many people become roommates after being together for so long, but the fire was extinguished many years back. This is not an uncommon situation; many couples agree to stay together in spite of the lost of romance. This is something that has to be worked on in order to reignite the flames. Perhaps they might consider going out on dates again and doing the unexpected.

THE AGING PROCESS OF THE BODY

In the previous segment I was speaking of how couples should grow together with time once they get to know each other very well. There are very little surprises after many years of marriage. With seasoning, you eventually let down most of the walls that you held on to for as long as possible. When you see a couple that has been together for a long time they almost seem to take on each other's character. They start finishing each other's sentences. With aging and familiarity there is comfort in knowing what to expect from the other party. However, there is another aging process that all bodies will face if people live long enough.

There were things you did when you were young that you cannot do when you are older. Relationships have to make these adjustments. People require medical attention or medication more often, and they need their partner to stand by them through such times. It is nice to have someone who has stood by your side through the years and is willing to stay there no matter what. Unfortunately, you don't seem to see as many people who mate for life like some of the older couples. A *real man,* no matter how old he becomes, would be there for his mate through thick and thin, for better or worse, because that is part of his character. Character should get better with age.

REACH FOR THE STARS

Young men need a star that they can aspire to reach. They need to be constantly improving and growing as individuals. As his family grows, so does his responsibilities; he needs to constantly mature in order to keep up with the expansion. If his responsibilities grow faster than his capabilities, something is bound to break. If he constantly reaches for the stars, he can stay out ahead of things and be ready to handle the challenges that come along. This can be achieved by setting goals and making plans that will keep you growing and motivated. Once you stop growing many things happen, most of them are not good. Reach for the stars and you may have to settle somewhere out on a distant planet. At least you are not still sitting back in the same boring place where it all started.

One of the major problems of males today is stagnation. Males have become complacent on the wrong side of the eight ball (progress). There are some who do the same things that they have always done to the point that their favorite chair has their body imprint etched into the fabric. Many men become creatures of habit and fail to see a huge ditch forming. If they continue on the current path, (doing nothing) they will continue to decline in overall net value to society. Everything about this situation is extremely correctable, but only the choice of doing nothing is the kiss of death.

Men can work as individuals, taking their own family members and leading them to safety. They can also work in small or large groups and make larger dents in their communities. Well established organizations such as churches, temples, or religious organizations can lead the charge to effect change. Civic and governmental agencies are already doing things to make resources available to those who know how to utilize their resources. Groups such as the boys and girls clubs, boy and girl scouts, mentor groups, and the like, are doing a great job of leading and caring for the children. If a man has no plan, all he would need to do is join an organization that is already functioning. Much is being done already, but much more can and should be done.

We are partly in this current predicament because we were waiting on someone else to take the ball and run. That someone is you. Everybody else is waiting on you to run with the ball. Take the ball and run in every way you know how and rest assured the problem will be tackled. Change starts at home; if anyone else chooses to participate all the better. If everyone reaches as high, or as far as is possible, we would have very few problems that bind us. A *real man* accepts this as his cross to bear. Upon his shoulders sits the fate of the world. If he fails, the world will suffer a loss. It is not that the entire world will crumble, because he is only responsible for what God has placed upon his plate. Anything more is the gravy for others to share. A real man thinks *gravy* rather than *barely enough to survive*. Reach for the stars fellows.

Chapter Twelve

IT'S ALL UP TO YOU

When you really think about the situation, this is your time in the spotlight. This is the time that fate, God, or whatever source placed you here on the planet. You could have been born during the cave man days, in the primitive jungle, during the dark ages, during a time of major wars, or you could have been born to live your days on earth right in this moment. Since that is certainly the case because you are currently here, think about what you can do with what you were given. If you measure your value by what you personally gain it places certain limitations upon you. If you are fortunate to be rich and famous there is much you can do with your name, fame and money. If you are not as fortunate, what is it that you can offer? The answer is simple, you can offer all you are as a man and hopefully that will be an improvement upon someone's life.

Desire comes from the heart. If you desire to be of assistance your heart will reach into the spiritual arena and manifest such things. If you desire to achieve personal gains from the heart, that power is available to us. It is from the heart that we manifest things. The stronger the desire the better we are at manifesting things. If you are not aware of such powers then this would certainly be an obtainable goal to investigate. If you research the lives of most successful people you will find that they all practiced a very powerful secret that eventually manifested their dreams. That main ingredient was faith. It was the belief that what they desired was possible. When that desire becomes strong in their hearts it made things happen. The problem with most people is the lack of faith or belief. If you do not believe you can achieve things, chances are you will not manifest what you seek.

Christ said it this way, "if you had the faith of a tiny mustard seed you could tell a mountain to leap into the sea and it would do it."

Although this may sound like gibberish, or religious hogwash, it is truer than you could imagine. The secret to achieving our goals is already hidden in us; all we need to do is activate the power that has been placed within us at birth. Therefore the power is already within your control. It is up to you to decide when or how to make the next move.

Please note that several suggestions, ideas, reference points, or even points of contention have been made in this material. As is customary, talk is very cheap, but action requires doing things. If any person is interested in becoming a positive element to society certainly there is enough mentioned in this quick book that can make a difference if implemented. In addition, you are encouraged to come up with your own ideas regarding formulating helpful ideas to improve upon what you may perceive as a potential cure to a particular problem.

Even though this book has used a minimum of research, it certainly did not explore all the available knowledge that is assessable. The intent here was to expose a potential problem and to ignite a fire under males in order to start the ball rolling. Certainly there are people who have a better insight upon the problem who are bringing their findings to the forefront as well. This situation has worldwide implications and should be dealt with from the broader prospective, rather than one writer's opinion.

Fortunately, this concern has been streaming through the universal waves of consciousness and several people are addressing this potential problem at the same time. If more people could combine resources the issues could be addressed on a broader scale. Instead of individuals teaching at least one more – it could be groups and organizations moving with a much broader brushstroke. Of those who are addressing the situation, most have the intent of correcting the problem rather than achieving personal gains. Because of this, anyone interested in joining the cause are encouraged to join forces with others who are already addressing the issues. Again, this places the ball back in your court.

Please be informed as well, that even though this book was written for males and addressing the situation primarily from a male prospective, if all things go according to the status quo, more females will be reading this book than males. This is because reading is not as high on the list of priorities for the average male as it is for females. Since women are essentially in the same fish bowl (macrocosm) as males, it would be as beneficial for them to read this material and encourage their mates to engage. Whatever it takes to get males to become more engaged in the picture is what needs to happen. If a little friendly persuasion can get more males to start paying attention and making changes, then that would be to the benefit of all.

At the same time there are women who are addressing the problem from the opposite point of view. Women have a vested interest in seeing men improve. What female would not want to see her man standing firm in his manhood and doing what he does best to make his mate feel secure? As males go so does society. The ball is in our court.

While we are addressing this new era in our evolutionary process, take the time to throw away the old before you fill in the new. Old mindsets and dysfunctional behaviors that have not served the greater good should be tossed into the trash bins. Why do we hold on to things that we know do not work? This is still a mystery! Perhaps we feel that it is better to have something, even if it does not work, rather than nothing at all. This is not a good policy. If something is ineffective it pulls against you like extra and unnecessary weight. This is like taking a mountain hike carrying an extra 25 pounds that you don't need. Strip yourself of the access baggage and your plight will be much more manageable. You are the only one who can make that decision with certainty. The ball is in your court.

For as long as is necessary, you may want to separate yourself from the masses long enough to analyze the situation and cut excess baggage. If you keep doing the same things that you have always done with the same people that you have always done these things with…you will not see change. If you are happy with your life as it is, then don't change it. If you see room for improvement, give yourself the empty thinking space in order to see things more clearly and then make changes accordingly. If this means taking your personal space back momentarily from your associates… certainly your real friends and associates will not mind you making changes that are to your benefit. If someone wants to hold you back or wish that you to remain the same...I would question their friendship. If they are placing their needs above yours, that is only natural, but if they are attempting to hold you back so that can advance ahead of you, then you need to put them into the excess baggage bins. If something was truly intended for you don't be afraid to let it go freely. If it returns you will know that it was intended for you. If not then shed the baggage. The ball is in your court.

As I write this final chapter, it feels as though I am preaching a sermon. It is not my intent to preach to or at you. It is merely my intent to awaken the higher part of you so it can speak to the lower part and encourage the real self to do what is necessary, and/or what is more beneficial. When people change, the signal normally comes from a source that is the higher self. The ability to change exists within and not necessarily because of forces that appear on the outside. Real and substantial change comes from within you, while temporary and lesser change comes from without. It is up to you to decide the kind of change you want for yourself and for all those who are attached to your manhood as well. Again, you know where the ball is when you are ready. Why settle for the common, ordinary, garden variety of a man when you can be a REAL MAN? THE BALL...

Epilogue

When I sat down to write this book I assumed it would be much longer and much more technical. As it turns out, most men don't want to use their brains more than necessary. If they (we) can get what they want without spending too much brain power - all the better! Although there is much more that could be said about this topic, enough has been said to make the point. Besides, a book of this size will usually encourage more men to start and finish a reading project. It is my hope as the writer that men will actually take this subject seriously and start implementing things to ensure they (we) are properly doing all that is possible in order to cover their manly responsibilities.

As this book is going to being published, a company by the same name is being formed. The intent is to have the book as an additional resource for males to capture the entire picture, rather than trying to cram all this knowledge into a few hours of group meetings. Although both cover much of the same material, the book is available to take home and read in an environment more suitable for absorbing the information at the reader's preferred learning curve. With that stated, be on the lookout for a *Real Men Seminar* coming to an area near you in the near future, or visit our website for current events and resources.

We have so much wisdom already fully contained in each of us that can be shared with our brothers in order to assist them in dealing with real-life issues they will surely face. This rich resource is basically free for the sharing when men come together in the spirit of helping each other to become better men. The long range goal is to set up all-male meeting groups in your communities and neighborhoods, so men can come together in small or large groups and gain a wealth of wisdom that other men already have within them. As men learn to break down these walls we have placed up as ego barriers we can accomplish much in return.

Even though this problem among males is huge, it is not insurmountable. All it takes is for men to become aware that a potential problem is on the horizon that needs our immediate attention.

Once we properly address the situation, all that would be needed is to follow through with the solutions that you learn at the meetings. When you take personal responsibility for yourself, and all who are depending upon your manhood, you would have made a dent in the only world that is within your control. You can't change how others deal with their problems, but you certainly can change how you deal with your own. If we change our world one person at a time, you would be amazed how far and how deep those changes would impact the entire world in a relatively short period of time. When you are ready you know where the ball is, so boldly go out and pick it up – then run with all the gusto you can muster.

Don't settle for anything less that becoming an authentic REAL MAN. By now I am sure you have a pretty good indication of what that entails. Selah!

ABOUT THE AUTHOR

Greg started his writing career during the fall of 1999 by keeping a journal of his daily life, including his thoughts and dreams. This journaling became somewhat of a habit of recording his daily events until it eventually evolved into a revelation of his spiritual findings and growth as well. He began to wonder why we are as we are, and what the cause of all things in the universe was. He wondered about God, the existence of a soul, and how all this universal cosmology works. Those deep thoughts became his first book. It was just a collection of notes journaling his newfound spirituality. It was titled, "In Search of the Soul." After the first book came many, many more. He caught the "writing bug", which never went away. It was as though a doorway had opened to another realm of consciousness. "Where were those thoughts coming from," Greg wondered? Today after, several dozen written manuscripts, his talent to write and deal with a variety issues has become second nature. A writer writes – that defines this author.

After you reach a certain age of maturity you can look back over your shoulders and see what life had purposed for you all along. There are many indicators leading to your divine purpose, but not all people are able to properly receive the signals. Perhaps you may have ended up partially achieving that purpose, but if there was no conscious connection between you (the receiver) and the Source from which it came, little may have been gained.

We are always receiving subliminal signals through subconscious or unconscious receptive modes. However, to do so in the conscious mode gives you more latitude and (connect-ability) awareness. Once you voluntarily connect with this Source, harmony is achieved between the Maker and the made. There is agreement in purpose and likeness – in desires and thought. Becoming one with God and His purposes is the ultimate gain. Throughout your entire life God has always been guiding you and sending you divine signals. It is up to the individuals to respond to His (lead) transmissions.

Being born during the summer of 1949 in Memphis Tennessee placed this writer on a certain directional path. His cultural experiences, such as dealing with racial and gender segregation, along with the rapid changes in technology, painted such a broad picture that most people rarely see. It is each person's life experiences that make them into the person they become. As you read this writer, you can sense the many slices of his life. Most of the dramatic shifts that are highlighted in this book came about during Greg's lifetime. The entire baby boomer generation has had a front row seat witnessing these changes.

In addition, the years of family life have also molded Greg into the man he has become today. His family has been an essential part of his credentials and purpose in becoming a real man. By providing, protecting, teaching, and learning from them, Greg found out that his ability to become a fully functional male was expressed more in others and not just in himself. "No *real man* is truly an island on this planet, nor was he intended to be so," says Greg.

He is not only a husband and father but also a grandfather to eight grandchildren. He's been with his wife Cynthia for 28 years; married to her for over 25 years. Both Greg and Cynthia had children prior to their union. Greg is also a part of a larger male experience as a son, brother, uncle, godfather, mentor, and friend. A lifetime within all these roles brought a wealth and wisdom of experience to Greg's life; wisdom he wishes to share with others. -Alyson Kay-

Real Men Seminars, LLC

In addition to being a writer, Greg Middleton is the founder of a business called "Real Men Seminars." This business was inspired by the need to address an escalating problem in the male gender as addressed in this book as well. By gathering males in an environment where they feel comfortable expressing their thoughts and feelings about many life issues and experiences, most men walk away with a new awareness. Previously, they may have felt that they were alone on certain issues, but after hearing the testimonies of other males they find more similarity. They learn that males were born differently by design opposed to how females were designed to function and operate. Once you understand the differences and incorporate that knowledge into your relationships it makes life more manageable.

At Real Men Seminars (RMS) we address many of the key issues that most men face in common to various degrees. These issues are addressed in our live seminars (all-male discussion groups) to a point where all men walk away with more knowledge than they entered with. Just grasping the difference between the male/female dynamic is in itself is an awakening experience. Some of the key issues the seminars deal with are:

- Understanding the male/female dynamic, needs, wants, and/or requirements.
- Learning to properly communicate with your mates.
- Dealing with domestic violence issues (anger management)
- Substance abuse issues; drugs, alcohol, prescription dependencies, sexual abuse…
- Fatherhood – parenting your children – paternal responsibilities in or out of marriage
- Criminal activities – placing your dependants at risk of loss of an effective parent.
- Men's dysfunctional attitudes about dealing with their health.

- Properly handling financial responsibilities.
- Marriage and divorce issues
- Infidelity issues – learning how to manage your sexual desires
- Addressing the rite of passage issues with young males…
- Mentoring our young and even older males in positive strides.
- 24-hour hotlines for immediate help (cooling down period) in domestic violence cases.

In addition, a website has been setup where men can visit in order to get assistance or direction as to where to go to get help in dealing with their issues. At this site our visitors may read vital information the affects males currently. If men are to improve themselves they must keep adequately informed. In addition to the live seminars and male-only discussion groups, we want to team up with other organizations that are addressing the same or similar problems. It certainly takes a village to raise a child. The more we get our communities involved, the better we will be served as people; males, females, children, and/or senior citizens: all will gain when the issues of our males are handled. Real Men Seminars is a venue where men can come together in order to assist each other in becoming better men. www.realmenseminars.com

OTHER PUBLISHED MATERIAL
BY GREG MIDDLETON

1. **In Search of the Soul** - *"A Soulful Search"* – Published 2002 by Dorrance Publishing Company, Inc. 643 Smithfield Street, Pittsburgh, Pennsylvania 15222 U.S.A. Phone 1 800-788-7654 ISBN # 0-8059-5476-5517-8

   In Search of the Soul - was this author's first published book. It was not originally intended to become a book but as fate would have it, it became the first of many more to come. Many people are searching for a deeper meaning in their lives, and Greg Middleton was certainly one of those. In Search of the Soul takes you along his spiritual journey. The book, which started out as Middleton's own diary, candidly shares his thoughts, his feelings and his progression. His gradual awareness eventually leads him to a deeper relationship with God.

2. **Pearls of Wisdom** – *a collection of spiritual essays*. Self-Published 2003 by GEM Publications, Altadena CA 91001. Phone 1 626-791-2770 ISBN # 0-9742354-0-7. Website: www.gregemiddleton.com

   This is a collection of spiritual essays written in a conversational style. It is the type of book that doesn't require reading from cover to cover because each essay has its own completion. Throughout the book you will find scriptural quotes that bring wisdom into the conversations. Every episode of our lives can be dealt with by applying the word of God to all we do and think. Each essay integrates spiritual messages and observations about seemingly ordinary everyday experiences.

3. **Food for the Soul** – Published 2005 by Cold Tree Press, Nashville Tennessee. ISBN #1-58385-072-4. Contact us for ordering this book. This book is now available through GEM Publications and can be ordered directly through Amazon or many other standard online book orders.

Just as you wouldn't abstain from feeding your body over long periods of time, neither should you abstain from feeding your soul. This book neatly packages vital nutrients from the Bible that your soul needs in order to thrive. Whether you are a Christian or anyone seeking greater understanding of the Bible, this book can assist you. It's God's word made easy. It explains many hidden secrets (that are not secret) hidden in the Bible. The book was written for Christian believers.

4. **Living Christianity** – Published 2006 by Cold Tree Press, Nashville Tennessee. ISBN #1-58385-158-5. Contact us for ordering this book.

Many people call themselves a "Christian" and for the most part truly believe that is what they are, however when it comes to actually living by the teachings of Christ - that is a different matter. In this book Middleton talks very straight forwardly about what it actually takes to live the Christian life according to what Christ taught. Christians are required to live to a higher moral standard than the world holds. Things you did while living under the power of sin are no longer acceptable. Using the power of the Holy Spirit we transcend our sin nature and become a new creation reshaped in the likeness of Christ. He (the Holy Spirit) will chastise you when you stray into darkness and embrace you when you require godly assistance (grace). This book is biblically based along with scriptural references. It will challenge you to raise your bar of expectation for yourself. The author asks that you stop trying to be a Christian but instead to become one. Live the Christian life. Walk the Christian walk.

5. **<u>The Seeker</u>** – A Path of Spiritual Awakening – Published 2009. This book may be purchased through Lulu.com book orders or Amazon.com and many other online book purchasing facilities.

This book is a slight deviation from the author's typical genre. Most of his earlier works were religious - specifically Christian. But, this one covers a wider audience and comes from a deeper prospective. Anyone can become a "Seeker" if they genuinely desire to learn what is available through the conscious signals that are always being emitted throughout the universe. "Seek and you shall find." However, if you seek from a specific source you will acquire specific knowledge from that source. You become the magnet that draws knowledge to you. If you seek from God then that is the Source of the wisdom and knowledge that you obtain.

In addition Middleton has a few websites where he regularly writes blogs and other inspirational messages. For more information about upcoming books or works, check the writer's official website. www.gregemiddleton.com

CONTACT INFORMATION

This information is to be provided prior to publishing.

Website www.gregemiddleton.com

Email contact information greg_middleton@att.net

Real Men Website: www.realmenseminars.com

Post Office mailing site:

P.O. Box 6304

Altadena, Ca 91003-6304